The Rookie's Guide
to the
Springfield Armory XD-S

The Rookie's Guide
to the Springfield Armory XD-S

What you need to know to buy, shoot and care for a
Springfield Armory XD-S

TOM MCHALE

First Edition
Insanely Practical Guides

Published by Insanely Practical Guides, Charleston, SC

Printed in the United States of America.

ISBN 978-0-9890652-5-2

Digital Edition ISBN 978-0-9890652-6-9

BUT FIRST, A SERIOUS NOTE

Proper handling and carrying of firearms is serious business. While we at Insanely Practical Guides aim (Ha! Pun intended!) to make the shooting world more accessible and understandable with a little humor now and then, we firmly believe that nothing takes the place of face-to-face, real-time training. So use this guide as an educational tool to help you understand some of the basics, but never substitute the contents of a quality publication like this one for the expert advice of a skilled and experienced firearms and personal defense trainer.

As this guide covers operation of specific products, the Springfield Armory XD-S pistols, please note that manufacturer instructions ALWAYS take precedence over information in this book. Manufacturers can change products and/or recommended procedures at any time, so always rely on their information first.

In true Insanely Practical Guides style, this book is written in literary assault format for your enjoyment — half-cocked but right on target. I hope that doesn't offend your sense of decency and decorum — too much.

Contents

The Springfield Armory XD-S: A Family Affair

Since the early 12th century, gun writers and internet ninja commandos have been arguing about which handgun cartridge is better - the 9mm or the .45 ACP.

Guess what?

There is no right answer to that question!

I love them both! And that's one of the reasons I wrote this book. You see, with the Springfield Armory XD-S you kind of get a two-for-one deal. I mean, you have to pay for both guns, but you can choose your favorite caliber, 9mm or .45 ACP, and get the same compact size and great features. If you believe in the ".45 ACP is king" theory, great! If you prefer more 9mm rounds in the same size gun, great! The Springfield Armory XD-S can please both.

With this book, you get a "buy-one, get-one-free" deal. Regardless of which model of Springfield Armory XD-S you're interested in, we'll teach you how to use it. You'll learn safe operation, proper maintenance, available accessories, holsters and ammunition. Heck, we even throw in some helpful shooting tips so you can look really impressive at the range.

If you've read any of my other books or articles, then you know I believe that learning can be fun - and that's how this book is written. The information is accurate and insanely practical, but I have an allergy to multi-syllable words, so I keep things simple and always in plain English.

If you own a Springfield Armory XD-S, or are thinking about getting one, then this book is for you! Read on!

INTRODUCING THE SPRINGFIELD ARMORY XD-S

When most companies develop a new pocket pistol, they start with a small caliber .380 ACP or maybe 9mm. Later on, they might "upsize" the new gun to handle a larger caliber like .40 S&W and sometimes even .45 ACP. Springfield Armory chose to drink the big gulp and launch their pocket-sized pistol in a big caliber - .45 ACP. Hey, go big or go home, right?

The neat thing about doing the big caliber first, other than rocking the gun market, is that once you have a frame and action that "fits" the larger caliber, it's a relatively straightforward process to implement a smaller caliber model.

At time of this writing, Springfield Armory offers two calibers in the XD-S family: .45 ACP and 9mm.

What's the "S" stand for? You might suggest "skinny" and you would be right - at least in an indirect sense. The "S" really stands for "single-stack" of the magazine design. Both the 9mm and .45 ACP versions have rounds stacked directly on top of each other. This allows for the skinniest possible overall design, although it does limit capacity.

You can't escape tradeoffs when it comes to size and capacity - something's gotta give. In this case, Springfield Armory chose to go for small size and concealability. When you look at what you get in the package, capacity becomes less of an issue, especially with the 9mm model.

SAME GUN, MULTIPLE CALIBERS

When I say same gun, I pretty much mean same gun. There are internal parts differences of course, but the exterior dimensions are identical in the .45 ACP and 9mm versions. As this book went to print, Springfield Armory announced the 9mm XD-S 4.0 model, which is still the same gun, except that it features a longer barrel - 4.0 inches instead of 3.3 inches. We'll talk more about what that does for your later.

Even key interior dimensions are the same between the two models. The magazine wells, and even the exterior of the magazines are the same width. The length (front to back) of the .45 ACP magazine is a bit longer due to the longer cartridge size, so you may need to account for that depending on what type of magazine carrier you use. Some are adjustable, others not so much.

While the magazines have the same "thickness," front to back dimensions are different.

I measure the thickness of the magazines at just about .558 inches. How's that you say? The .45 ACP is much thicker than the 9mm! If you take a close look at the magazines, you'll see that they are shaped to create interior differences. The 9mm magazines have ridges pressed into the sides that account for the narrower diameter of the 9mm cartridge. Clever eh?

The Springfield Armory XD-S is currently offered in .45 ACP (left) and 9mm (right). We're betting a .40 S&W version will appear at some point. Both current models are available in all black or two-tone finish.

The only observable difference between the two, excepting the caliber marking, is the thickness of the barrel. We'll get to that in a minute.

For now, just know that any holsters and accessories you have for one work equally well on the other. The only possible exception is the new 9mm XD-S 4.0 model, which has a longer slide and barrel than the original.

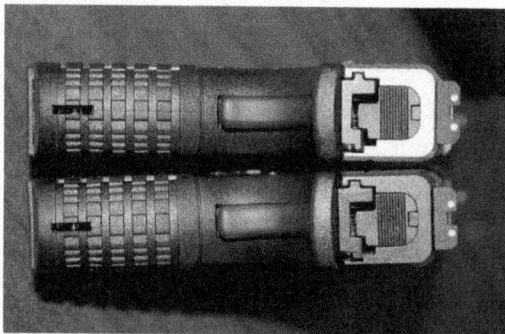

Can you tell which is which?

Now that I've gone on and on about how similar these guns are, let's point out the differences.

Even the brand new XD-S 4.0 shares the same frame body as the other models. Just the barrel and slide are longer.

THE XD-S 9MM VS. THE XD-S .45 ACP

The primary difference is capacity, and that's simply a result of the 9mm cartridge being skinnier than that big fat .45 ACP. You can fit more skinny clowns into a Volkswagen Beetle than fat ones. It's the same with cartridges and magazines.

The standard magazine of the 9mm model holds seven rounds while the .45 ACP model holds five. Including a cartridge in the chamber, that's eight and six respectively. Both pistols have an optional extended magazine that adds additional grip length. The longer magazine brings 9mm capacity to nine plus one in the chamber and .45 ACP model capacity to seven plus one.

You might wonder why the 9mm version is 1 ½ ounces heavier than the .45 ACP model. That seems a little backwards doesn't it? From my observations, the exterior barrel diameter is the same for both calibers, but of course the interior diameter of the 9mm model is smaller. Therefore, the barrel of the 9mm model is "thicker" and a bit heavier.

Here's why the 9mm model is a bit heavier. The exterior dimension of the barrels of the .45 ACP and 9mm are the same. The 9mm has a smaller bore, so the barrel walls are thicker. That extra metal is heavy, hence the difference!

WHICH ONE IS RIGHT FOR YOU?

Which one is right for you depends...

Not too long ago, when you needed to choose a caliber that had the best chance of stopping a determined attacker quickly, bigger was perceived to be better. Today, ammunition makers are doing fantastic things to increase the performance of their products. Modern hollow point ammunition is designed to expand (squish flatter and increase in diameter) when it hits a flesh target, thereby increasing likelihood of stopping a threat quickly.

We're not going to get into a ballistic effectiveness theory dissertation here. Just realize that the 9mm round has proven itself a great self-defense performer. Much of the "old wisdom" comparing 9mm to .45 ACP is a carryover from the days of full metal jacket (non-expanding) bullets. In those cases, 9mm tends to make little holes and pass right through targets, while .45 ACP makes bigger holes at lower velocity.

With modern ammunition, you might see a 9mm (.355 inch diameter) projectile expand to somewhere around .53 inches diameter. A .45 ACP projectile might expand to .67 inches give or take a bit.

So what does that .14 inch diameter difference really mean? If you filter out the internet opinions about one or the other, and look at mountains of police shooting data, you'll see that the effectiveness data between 9mm and .45 ACP is practically the same. The percentages of bad guys who are stopped with a single shot are about equal between the two. The average number of shots required to stop an attacker are also about equal. Bottom line? Other factors, like shot placement, matter a whole lot more than choice of caliber.

So don't get hung up on the 9mm vs. 45 ACP debate - they both make excellent self-defense calibers, provided you use quality self-defense ammunition.

When picking which Springfield Armory XD-S is right for you, consider how it shoots and how it feels in your hand when you shoot it. Do you have preference for the recoil "feel" of one versus the other? The .45 ACP will certainly provide more of a "push" but that may not matter to you.

The other thing to consider is the capacity. Do you feel "comfortable" with the six rounds in the .45 ACP model? Or do you have a bit more peace of mind with the eight round 9mm?

The standard and optional extended 9mm magazines hold seven and nine rounds, respectively.

One more consideration to add to the mix is ammunition cost. Your self-defense ammunition won't really matter, because you won't shoot that very often. Practice ammo does have a price difference between 9mm and .45 ACP, with the .45 being somewhat more expensive on a per-round basis.

What did I choose? I couldn't decide, so I bought both! Since the dimensions are the same, I can share holsters and pick up whichever one strikes me as appropriate for that day. On a day to day basis, I don't tend to favor one over the other - they both get about the same amount of use.

A Guided Tour

Getting To Know Your Springfield Armory XD-S

If you haven't already bought a Springfield Armory XD-S, you're in for a treat! You'll find that the Springfield Armory XD-S is elegantly machined, polished and fit. Simply put, it's a fine piece of equipment.

WHAT YOU GET IN THE BOX

The case

The first thing you get in the case is... the case itself! The XD-S is packaged in a traditional Springfield Armory hard case with foam inserts for each component. One thing about Springfield Armory gun cases - they are fantastic. You would normally pay more than chump change for a case like this.

What's this for? We're not exactly sure, but it looks tactical.

The case has tactical rails on each side, but quite frankly, we don't know why. I suppose you could store a light, laser or pistol bayonet on the case when not in use. Rumor has it that some magazine loaders have rail attachments, so you could keep that neatly stored while shooting. A call to Springfield Armory yielded the mysterious answer of... "you'll see soon." So, enjoy the aesthetics and see if you can come up with a good use for the rails.

The case features two solid latches and two holes for locks, so it's TSA friendly. Air travel with a gun requires a solid, lockable case and this one is ready to fly. As always, check with your specific airline before showing up at the airport, but as of this writing, this case is good to go as long as you add your own external locks.

Springfield Armory does an excellent job of packaging. The XD-S comes in a hard case with perfectly cut foam for the gun, magazines and included accessories.

Inside the case is everything you need to start shooting, except the ammunition. Most Springfield Armory products are not the least expensive kids on the block, but you get what you pay for.

The XD-S comes with a complete carry setup.

The Springfield Armory XD-S comes with everything you need to get started: Extra magazines, a dual maga-zine carrier and a holster. Not shown: Safety lock, owners manual, alternate size back strap and spare fiber optic tubes. Check when you buy as not all packaging options include the extended magazine shown here.

Spare magazine

Springfield Armory includes a second magazine right in the box. If you want the extended magazine shown throughout this book, that's an optional accessory that you can buy online from Springfield Armory or nearly any gun retailer.

The paddle-style holster carriers the XD-S outside the waistband.

Holster

One of the extras you get with the Springfield Armory XD-S is a serviceable carry holster. It's a paddle design, meaning you can slip it on over your pants and belt - no need to plan ahead and wind your belt through loops.

Like any other design, paddle holsters have advantages and disadvantages. You can easily put on, and remove, a paddle holster at various times of the day. If your daily routine takes you to places where guns are prohibited, you can easily and safely remove your gun and holster. Just remove the whole assembly together. There's no need to take your gun out of the holster to take the holster off or put it back on.

An adjustable retention screw allows you to adjust the "tightness" of the gun / holster fit.

On the flip side, it's possible for paddle holsters to come out while drawing your gun. The Springfield Armory XD-S paddle holster includes an aggressive "shelf" that is designed to press through your pants and under the bottom of the belt. This is intended to help keep the paddle holster down while the gun is drawn upwards. It works pretty well provided you use a proper belt. Just be aware that no paddle holster will provide the same level of security to your belt as a loop style holster.

The paddle slips over your belt and inside the pants. The hook helps keep the holster in place when you draw the gun - it catches on the bottom of your belt when mounted properly.

The holster itself offers good retention for the XD-S. The trigger guard area is molded with a small indent that helps hold the gun in the holster. There is also an adjustable retention screw that allows you to increase the overall friction pressure that retains the pistol.

With a carefully inspected unloaded gun, draw the gun from the holster a number of times to help break it in. Then experiment with the retention screw to find the level of hold you like.

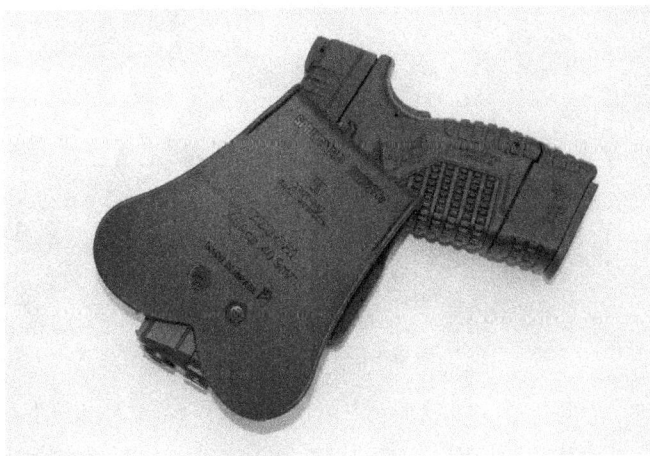

The paddle itself rides against your body - and is large and smooth for stability and comfort.

Magazine carrier

A dual magazine carrier is included. Rails on both sides of the carrier allow you to mount other gizmos like lights (when not in use) or rail mounted laser sights.

Due to the front to back length difference of the .45 ACP and 9mm magazines, Springfield Armory provides magazine holders for each model. Functionally they're identical, the magazine holes are just shaped every so slightly larger for the .45 ACP model.

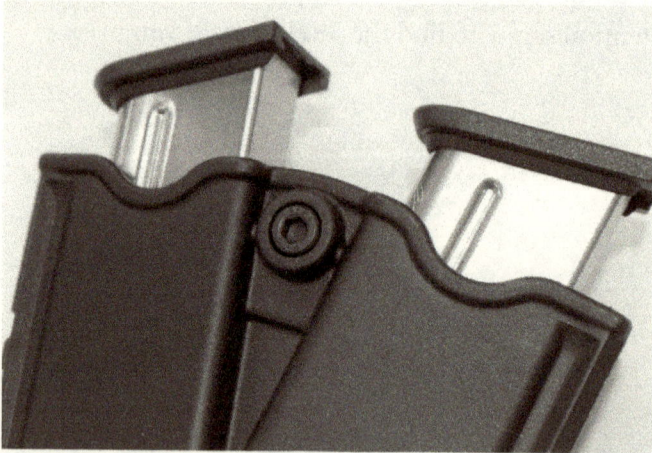

The retention screw adjustment allows you to seat magazines in the carrier as firm, or as loose, as you wish.

The included magazine carrier uses two molded belt loops for outside the waistband carry. The magazines are angled slightly away from each other to aid in access. I find that this helps a bit with concealment too as the angle profiles tends to follow your body.

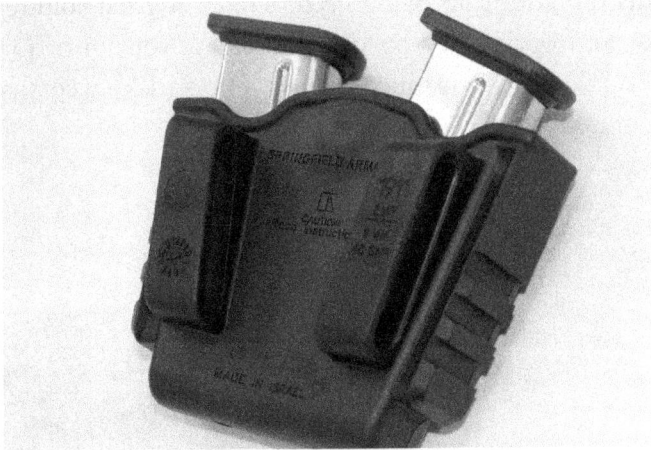

You feed your belt through two polymer loops that are molded into the magazine carrier.

The magazine carrier works great with belts up to 1 ½ inches in width. Depending on your belt and the material its made of, you might be able to squeeze a 1 ¾ inch belt through there too.

As with the holster, there's an included retention screw so you can decide how tight you want the magazines held in place.

Alternate back strap

One of the features of the XD-S is a changeable back strap. This allows you to adjust the circumference of the grip to best fit your hand. In addition to the back strap already on the pistol, Springfield Armory includes a larger one should you want to adjust the fit.

Safety lock

Like most modern handgun companies, Springfield Armory provides a lock that will disable operation of the gun. This one is a padlock with a cable. Simply remove the magazine, open the action, being certain there is no cartridge in the chamber, and run the cable through the magazine well as shown here. Lock it up and secure the keys somewhere safe. This is a simple and effective solution that prevents the gun from being fired. This is a great solution for storage, but not appropriate if you need to access your gun quickly. For that scenario, you may want to check out quick access safes like the GunVault.

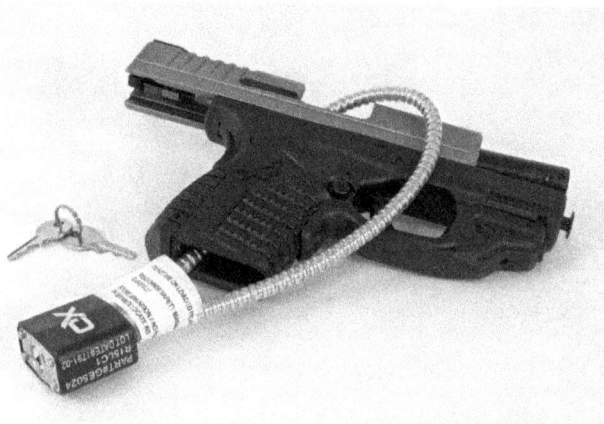

While simple, the lock effectively prevents the XD-S from being fired.

Miscellaneous tools and parts

Springfield Armory includes a stiff nylon cleaning brush on a braided wire handle right in the box. You can use this for rudimentary cleaning, but sooner or later, you'll want a proper cleaning kit like the OTIS Technology kit discussed later in this book.

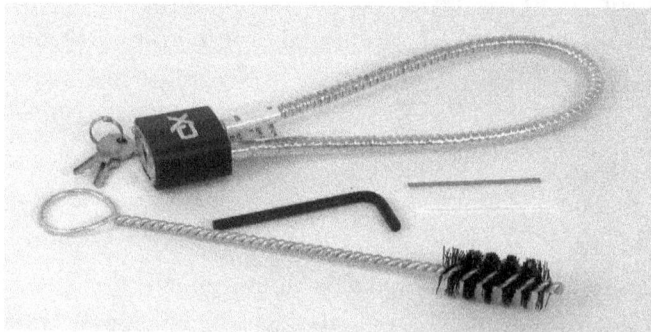

A few of the extras included with the Springfield Armory XD-S

There is also an allen wrench that fits the retention screws on the included holster and magazine carrier. That's a nice touch!

Springfield Armory also includes spare fiber optic rod material for the front sight. The pistol comes with a red fiber optic front sight, but if you prefer green, there is an extra rod that you can install in minutes. There's also spare red fiber optic rod material should you damage the pre-installed sight.

Springfield Armory XD-S pistols are made in Croatia. The attention to detail with fit and finish shows that those folks know how to make a quality gun!

FEATURES

Let's take a look at the various features of the Springfield Armory XD-S and examine their purpose and value.

Grip Safety

Like the famous 1911 design, the Springfield Armory XD-S features a grip safety. The idea behind a grip safety is that you never need to worry about it - it's there, in part, to make sure that the trigger cannot be depressed unless the gun is in a proper firing grip. Taking a normal and proper grip on your pistol will deactivate the grip safety as the web of your hand will push it into the grip frame, thereby allowing the gun to fire.

The grip safety is depressed by the web of your hand when you assume a firing grip.

Ultra Safety Assurance (USA) trigger system

We'll talk more about this when we get to the section on how to safely operate your Springfield Armory XD-S. For now, just make a note of that little lever in the trigger face. Unless that is depressed, the trigger won't move. This helps protect against undesired discharges from dropping the gun or a foreign object pressing against the side of the trigger.

Fail safe disassembly

The XD-S has a built-in reminder to unload the gun before taking it apart for field-stripping and maintenance. That is, the magazine must be removed in order for the takedown lever to even operate. We'll cover this in detail a little later when we discuss how to clean and maintain the XD-S.

Ambidextrous magazine release

Many modern handguns brag about having a magazine release button that can be uninstalled from one side and reinstalled in the other. The purpose of a reversible design like that is to accommodate right and left-handed shooters.

Magazine release buttons are already present on both sides of the frame.

However, it does nothing to address the potential problem of suddenly having to switch hands while you're shooting. There are many reasons you might have, or want, to do this. You might need to shoot around a door or corner on your support side. You might have an injury on your normal side hand or arm. You might be holding a child with your strong arm. The list goes on.

Springfield Armory does it right and has both right and left side magazine release buttons already in place. Righty? Fine. Lefty? Fine. Need to switch hands while shooting? Fine. It's one of those "fit and finish" details I like so much about Springfield Armory products. They're a little more expensive than others, but when you start looking at all the small details, you'll see why.

Loaded chamber indicator

If you look on the top of the slide of the Springfield Armory XD-S, you'll see a thin piece of black metal just behind the barrel chamber. This is the loaded chamber indicator. It's a simple idea: if there is a cartridge in the chamber, it will press upwards on this metal strip and you will be able to both see and feel that it's in a raised position.

While unlikely, it's possible that there could be a spent cartridge casing in the chamber, and that would cause the loaded indicator to operate as well, so think of this feature as a "there's something in the chamber" indicator.

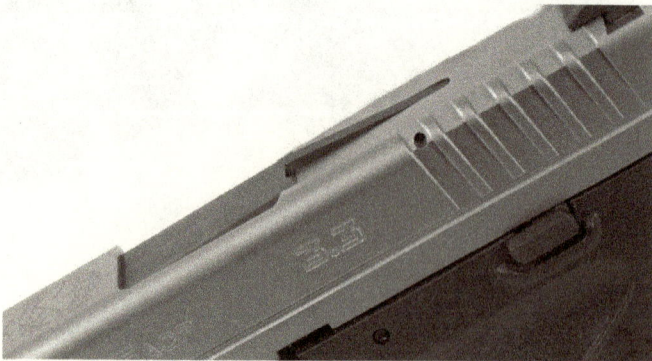

The loaded chamber rises out of the top of the frame when a cartridge is in the chamber.

Windage adjustable front and rear sights

That's kind of a weird description, isn't it? Windage? Like you'll have to adjust your sights on gusty days or something. In this context, windage simply means sideways. If you find that some combination of you, your ammo and your XD-S shoots a little left or right, you can adjust either the front or rear sight to make sure that the sights line up with your point of impact.

Be careful to make sure that the sights really do need adjusting before moving anything. Small guns especially are susceptible to shooter error like jerking the trigger!

We'll show you how to adjust your sights later in the Tips and Tricks chapter.

No-slip grip texture

One of the benefits of polymer frame handguns is that manufacturers can easily create most any texturing pattern imaginable - at relatively low cost.

The grip texture is aggressive, and we expected some hand abuse. We were pleasantly surprised with how comfortable the XD-S is to shoot. No bandaids required!

The pattern on the sides and front of the Springfield Armory XD-S grip resemble dozens of rectangular-base pyramids with the tops chopped off. This creates a good texture that resists sweaty-hand slippage, but with no sharp points to dig into your hands or sides if you're using a belt holster.

I've been shooting XD-S pistols here in the lowcountry of South Carolina where humidity reaches 3,412% and I find the grips very effective - even in obscenely sweaty conditions.

Fiber optic front sight

The fiber optic front sight makes a surprising difference in visibility. You're supposed to focus only on the front sight after all, so why not really make it stand out?

I find that 3 dot systems (one white dot in the front and two on the rear sight) are effective, but slower to pick up. When the front and rear sights look the same in terms of contrast, you really need to make a deliberate effort on the front sight.

Note how the top of the fiber optic tube is exposed to collect ambient light.

The fiber optic tubes are open on the top, allowing the fiber optic material to "collect" ambient light from the sun or even indoor lighting. When you look at the end of the tube, it literally glows except in very dark conditions. You'd think it was electrically powered. This sight really jumps out at you. Don't like the red? No problem, replace it with the green tube included in the box. We'll show you how to do that later in the book.

Melonite finish

Melonite is a marketing descriptor that refers to the process of *ferritic nitrocarburizing*. Although the name implies that this is a *carburizing* process, it's actually a *nitriding* process. Got that? Me either.

The layman's explanation is that this is a process of creating a penetrating finish on steel gun parts, like the slide and barrel on the XD-S. It's done by cooking the parts in a smokin' hot and very bubbly salt bath containing alkali cyanate. Think of taking a home aquarium, loading it up with toxic chemicals, heating it to a thousand degrees or so, then aerating the water with a jet engine and you've got the idea.

All of this simmering creates a two layer surface embedded into the steel which does three things: resists corrosion, creates a very, very hard and scratch-resistance surface and reduces friction.

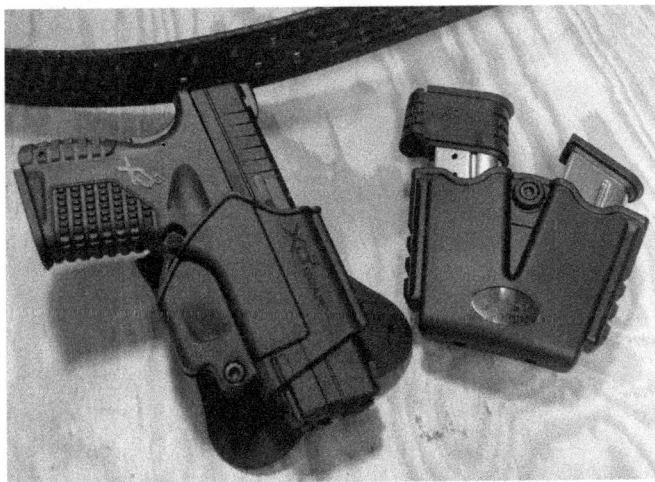

The entire slide and barrel assemblies are treated with Melonite on this finish. The two-tone XD-S has Melonite treatment on the barrel, but utilizes a brushed stainless steel finish on the slide.

So this is a good thing. The Melonite finish allows you to do things with your XD-S like carry it in your pants, and sweat all over it without rusting your pistol. It'll look good for years and years unless you royally abuse it. All those moving parts will continue to work smoothly.

Adjustable grip

In addition to the back strap that comes on the Springfield Armory XD-S, you'll find a second back strap insert. This allows you to configure the grip size of the XD-S to best fit your hand size.

The larger grip (installed here) can easily be replaced with a smaller one.

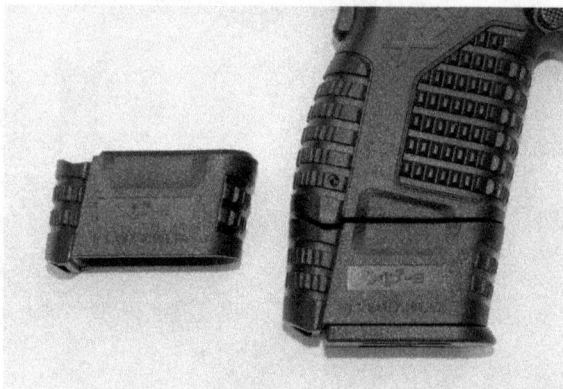

Springfield Armory even includes an alternate extended magazine sleeve when you buy that optional part. If you use the slimmer grip, then the extended magazine will still match up exactly.

Changing the grip size by replacing the back panels is a piece of cake. We'll cover that a little bit later on.

Shooting the XD-S

How to safely operate your Springfield Armory XD-S

> *"One of the primary advantages of compact defensive handguns like the XD-S is that you can have it with you all the time. You know about the First Rule of Gunfighting, right? HAVE A GUN! But this also means that seasonal or occasional clothing may not allow you to wear the gun in the same way every time. A gun like the XD-S can be carried on the belt, IWB, in a belly band, on the ankle, or in a pocket. This gives you a great deal of options for staying well-armed in lightweight summer clothing, a business suit, or even a tuxedo."*

> Mike Barham, Media and Public Relations Manager,
> Galco Gunleather

SAFETY FIRST!

The Springfield Armory XD-S is loaded with safety features. First, let's take a look at those designed to prevent the pistol from firing unless deliberate action is applied. Remember, no mechanical devices can, or should, take the place of strict adherence to the rules of gun safety. Those rules are so important, I've included a chapter on the four rules of gun safety.

Ultra Safety Assurance Action Trigger System. This fancy name simply refers to that little lever that sticks out from the face of the trigger. Unless that hinged lever is pressed, the trigger is locked. There are good reasons for this. It helps prevent an inertia-based trigger movement in the event you drop the pistol. It also minimizes the chance of trigger movement from side pressure originating from a holster or other obstruction. Basically, you need to properly apply your finger to the trigger face to deactivate this safety and press the trigger.

25

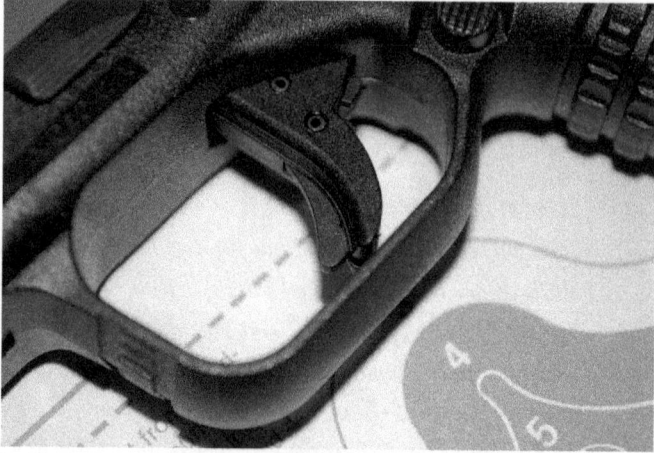

See that little lever in the center of the trigger face? Unless you press it, the trigger remains locked. With a proper and normal trigger press, you won't even notice it's there.

Grip Safety. Like the famous 1911 design, the Springfield Armory XD-S uses a grip safety that is depressed by the web of your hand when you take a proper firing grip. Until the grip safety is depressed, the trigger remains locked.

The grip safety adds another layer of protection. When you assume a proper firing grip, the trigger unlocks. Otherwise, the trigger remains locked.

Striker Block Safety. This one is a bit tricky as you can't see it without taking your XD-S apart. It's an internal safety that prevents the striker - the XD-S version of a firing pin - from moving towards the cartridge until both the grip safety and trigger safety are disengaged.

All of these safety mechanisms act as "layers" to help avoid unintentional discharges resulting from a dropped pistol or other artificial influence on the operation of the handgun. **None of these features will prevent negligent discharges - those resulting from someone pulling the trigger on a loaded gun**. Please read the Gun Safety Rules chapter as it details the four universal rules of gun safety. These are designed to prevent negligent discharges, The Owners Manual included with the Springfield Armory XD-S also provides excellent tips for safe operation of your gun.

HOW TO MAKE SURE YOUR XD-S FITS YOU

Earlier I mentioned that the Springfield Armory XD-S includes two back straps for the grip. So how do you know which one to use?

Comfort is a factor, but it's not a definitive method of fitting a handgun. Just because one grip or another "feels good" doesn't mean that you've got a proper fit. To be sure, you'll want to check two other things.

Trigger finger placement

Some experts will insist that you should press the trigger with the pad of your index finger. Other equally credible experts insist that you should use the first joint in your index finger. Some of the differences of opinion stem from the anticipated "style" of shooting. Are you at a range doing slow and methodical shots? Perhaps you plan to compete in a bullseye target competition? Or maybe you want to take up action shooting sports? Or maybe your interest is pure combat or self-defense. I don't particularly care which trigger press placement you prefer. Settle on one, then let's check to see if your guns grip size is too big or small.

With a very, very unloaded gun, assume a normal firing grip and point at a safe backstop. Now move your finger to the trigger as if you're going to fire. Hold that position.

I want you to look at the lower portion of your index finger - the area from where it plugs into your palm up to the first joint. When your trigger finger is ready to press, do you see daylight between the gun and your finger?

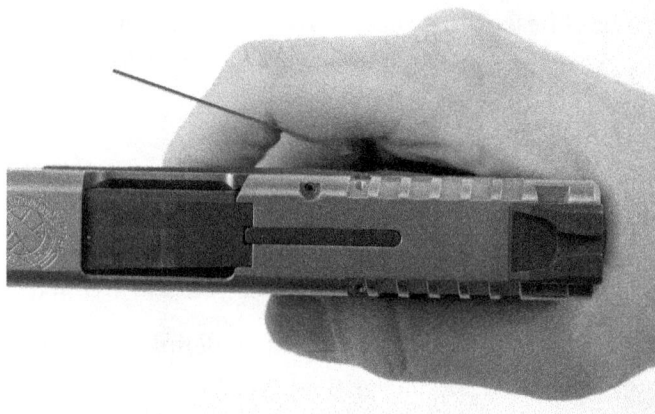

Notice the gap between my whole index finger and the side of the gun. If I press the trigger correctly, only the tip of my finger will move against the gun.

If your finger looks something like the picture here, you're good to go. If the bottom surface of your lower index finger is pressed against the side of the gun, you're having to reach for the trigger. This means that your grip is too large for your hand size. That matters because as you flex your finger to press the trigger, your index finger will be contacting the side of your gun and gently encouraging it to move off target! The good news is that if you're a lousy shot, you can blame the fit of your gun.

Alignment with your arm bone

This second test is a little less obvious. At the range, I see all sorts of shooters struggling with accuracy and ability to control recoil as a result of a crooked arm / gun relationship.

What does this mean? It's simple. When you hold your gun in a firing grip, with your trigger finger placed to pass test one above, the gun barrel should be in perfect alignment with your "radi-ulni." That's short hand for the two bones in your forearm - the radius and ulna. You don't just want the gun barrel to be parallel to these two bones, you want it to be a direct linear extension of these bones.

If your gun grip is too large for you, there will be a necessary tendency for you to grasp the gun so that the web of your hand wraps around towards the trigger, so your index finger can reach. This means that your thumb moves around and is directly behind the gun. Check out this picture to see an exaggerated view of what I mean.

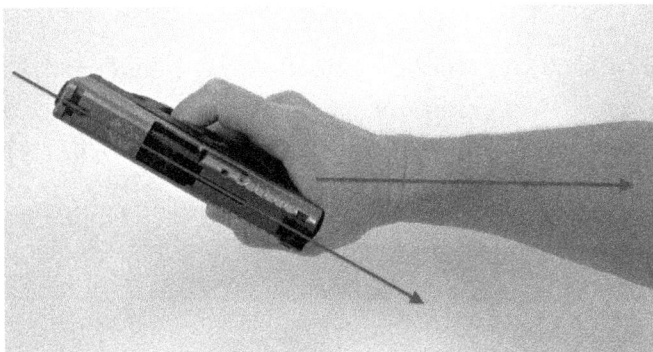

If you have to "reach around" the grip to get your finger on the trigger, you might end up supporting the back of the gun with your thumb! Note how the gun will recoil in a direction with no support.

With a properly fitted grip, you won't need to reach around to get proper access to the trigger. Your alignment will look more like this.

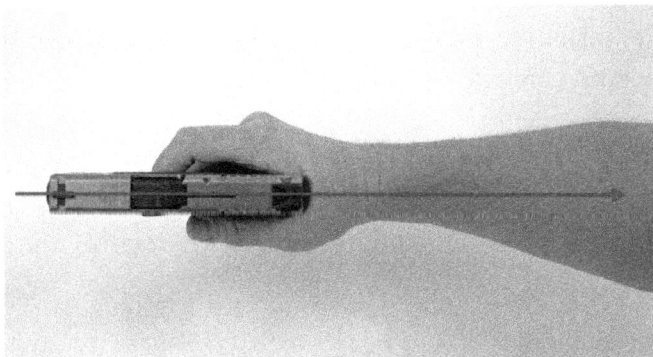

Here's what you want to see. Everything is in one straight line. You'll control recoil better and have a more natural ability to aim.

Why is this so important? In the first photo, you can see that when the gun recoils, it's going to press right against your thumb. There's not much body mass in your thumb to control that recoiling gun - even if you're all thumbs. You'll really feel that recoil. More importantly, your gun will be likely to jump radically off target with each shot.

By aligning the bigger and heavier parts of your body directly behind the recoil impulse of the pistol, your body mass controls the recoil. Additionally, the gun benefits from your natural pointing direction. If you close your eyes and try to point your fist at something, you'll notice that your arm bones end up pointed directly at your target. Why not make the gun a simple extension of that natural process?

So pick up your verified unloaded XD-S and try these two tests. If you struggle with either, put on the smaller grip panel and try again. We'll show you exactly how to change the grip size just a little later.

After all this testing, you may find that you can pass *both* tests with either grip back strap installed. Lucky you! Now you can choose whichever back strap option "feels" best. Better yet, try one for a week, then switch to the other. Then decide.

TRIGGER OPERATION

A few things have to happen in order for the XD-S trigger to operate:

1. The pistol has to be "cocked." As the Springfield Armory XD-S does not have a traditional hammer, this simply means that the slide has been pulled back and released, thereby applying tension to the striker. The XD-S will also be "cocked" automatically after each shot. It's easy to tell if your XD-S is in the cocked position - the trigger will remain back against the rear of the trigger guard area.

2. The grip safety has to be depressed. Don't worry, this happens automatically when you hold the pistol with a proper grip.

3. The trigger safety has to be pressed.

Your XD-S should have about ⅜ of an inch of take-up before the trigger releases. Take-up simply refers to the amount of travel in the trigger before you encounter resistance.

The trigger reset on the XD-S is designed to be short. This helps you to stay on target and fire repeat shots with minimum movement of the gun. After firing a shot, hold the trigger back against the rear of the trigger guard. Now, staying safely on target, slowly allow the trigger to move forward until you feel a distinct click. At this point, the firing mechanism is reset and you can pull the trigger again. You don't have to allow it to travel all the way forward for subsequent shots. On the two XD-S pistols covered in this book, the reset distance was only about ¼ of an inch.

HOW TO PROPERLY GRIP YOUR SPRINGFIELD ARMORY XD-S

This technique actually applies to just about any semi-automatic pistol. Revolvers can be a little different - we talk about that in *The Rookie's Guide to Guns and Shooting, Handgun Edition.*

So how do you achieve a proper handgun grip?

Step 1 is to grip the gun as high as possible. This will help control recoil, especially with a small gun like the XD-S.

With your primary shooting hand, open your thumb and index finger. Push the web of your hand as high as it will comfortably go on the handgun grip, making sure that the barrel of the gun lines up with the bones in your forearm.

Note how the firing hand is high on the gun and the fingers are placed high against the bottom of the trigger guard. The trigger finger is placed alongside of the slide for safety.

Wrap your fingers around the front of the grip, making sure to keep your index finger out of the trigger.

Your firing hand fingers should also be wrapped around the grip as high as possible.

Do you see some free space on the inside grip panel of your handgun? Good, that's where the bottom part of your support hand palm is going to go.

Try to place the meaty part of your palm, adjacent to your thumb, onto the side of the grip. Smack it on there and don't worry if there's not enough room to get your whole palm on the inside grip panel. There won't be and that's OK.

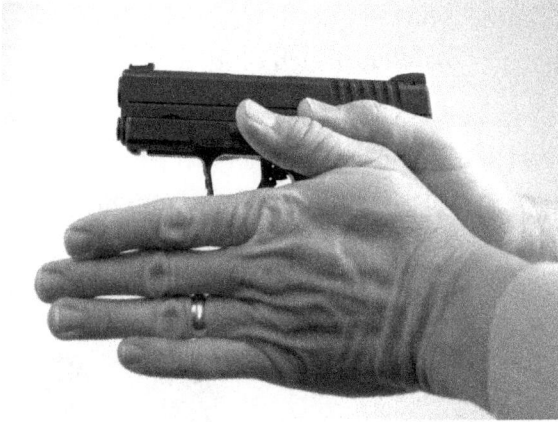

Press your palm against the support side of the grip.

Now wrap your support hand fingers around the front of the grip, making sure to place them as high as possible on the front strap of the grip. Your support hand index finger should be pressing against the bottom of the trigger guard.

Note how both thumbs are pointed forward. This is a solid grip!

The final product. Support fingers are right up against the trigger guard and both thumbs are facing forward.

Now wrap your support hand fingers around the front of your dominant hand fingers. Your support hand fingers should be high–to the point of pressing against the bottom of the trigger guard.

You'll know you've got it right if both of your thumbs are somewhere near parallel to each other and touching.

Next time you shoot, notice how much less your muzzle jumps. Your support hand can do wonders to help control recoil when you actually put it to work! Plus, a proper handgun grip looks really cool – you'll be a hit at the range. And those forward-facing thumbs? They naturally help you aim. Things tend to go where you point.

The extended magazine allows plenty of room for all fingers. While still thin and concealable, it's like shooting a full size pistol.

HOW TO BUILD A SOLID STANCE

While the movie Weekend at Bernie's qualifies as a cult movie and spawned it's own cool dance moves, it really doesn't play well at the range. Mainly because dancing tends to throw off your aim.

Doing the Bernie simply refers to leaning backwards from the waist, so your shoulders are behind your belt line. Your head also leans back, like you're trying to stop a nose bleed.

This tendency to lean backwards away from the gun has no practical value. You see, there is little chance that your gun will suddenly turn around and start chasing you, so the position really provides no tactical advantage.

Our model shooter is doin' the Bernie! Leaning away from the gun like this, she has little control over the gun and the recoil about to happen.

There are a couple of consequences to the Bernie lean that are pretty important. If you're already leaning backwards, you've given a big advantage to that recoil force that's about be applied to you. The bigger the gun, the more likely you are to be pushed off balance. Follow up shots are also more difficult as you have not provided a stable platform.

Speaking of stable platforms, semi-automatic pistols rely on the shooter pushing back against recoil force in order to operate correctly. The frame of a semi-automatic needs to be held stable in order for the slide and springs to do the work of ejecting a spent cartridge and loading a new one.

This is especially important with a compact gun like the Springfield Armory XD-S. And a solid grip and stance is yet more important with the .45 ACP XD-S than the 9mm XD-S. Smaller guns have a shorter recoil motion with which to eject the spent casing and chamber a new one.

You might hear about different styles of handgun stances like these:

The Weaver Stance: Place your support side foot forward of your shooting side foot. Put your shooting side arm straight out. Use your support hand to pull back on the gun, keeping your elbow bent, to create some isometric tension.

The Isosceles Stance: As the Sword of Damocles was made obsolete by guns, the Handgun Stance of Isosceles became cool. Keep both feet parallel to the target, shoulder width apart. Now shove both arms forward to form a triangle. That's where the "isosceles" part of Isosceles Stance comes from. Clever huh?

So which of these is right for you if you're going to ban the Bernie from your shooting? It doesn't make a darn bit of difference, because you can obtain a proper shooting stance with either of those methods– or some other.

Before worrying about the nuances of one technical stance over another, worry about getting your weight forward. It's pretty simple.

1. Place your feet about shoulder width apart.

2. If you like to put your weak side foot a little forward, great, do that.

3. If you prefer to keep your feet side by side, great, do that.

4. Flex your knees a bit. That makes the next step easier and gives you a better shock-absorbing platform. It also facilitates movement. Crazy things those knees!

5. Here's the important part. Bend a little forward at the waist. Your collarbone should be in front of your belt buckle. If you're not wearing a belt, pretend you are.

6. Roll your shoulders inward and down just a touch. That'll help control recoil even more.

7. Assume your Weaver, Isosceles, or Iron Lotus position. It doesn't matter.

8. Make sure those shoulders stay in front of your waist.

That's it!

Our shooter is not in complete control. Note how the eyes and shoulders are forward of the waist.

You see, when it comes to killing Bernie (yet again) most of the battle is getting your body weight forward. The nuances of arms and feet positions are secondary to that.

You'll be amazed at how little your handgun recoils when you get your weight forward of your belt. You'll make that gun your bit...

never mind. Let's just say you will be controlling your handgun–not the other way around.

After all, you never see Chuck Norris leaning away from those nameless henchmen do you?

The importance of trigger press with the Springfield Armory XD-S!

Why not just pull it?

The number one cause of misses is a poor trigger press. By listening to shooters at the range, you might assume that a lot of guns shoot low. Or high. Or a bit to the left. Or especially a bit to the lower left.

In reality, it's almost always the shooter, not the gun, causing shots to go high, low, left or right. What's the last thing to happen before the bullet leaves the barrel? That's right, pressing the trigger.

Notice we say "press" and not "pull." Pulling the trigger implies a rougher and more aggressive motion. Like a Yeti stomping through the woods. You rarely see a Yeti glide through the woods right?

Here's the issue. The Springfield Armory XD-S weighs about 1.5 pounds. It takes between 5.5 and 7.5 pounds of pressure to press the trigger on the XD-S. When you apply that 5.5 to 7.5 pounds of pressure, what tends to happen? Right, the gun wants to move!

With a compact handgun like the XD-S, you have to figure out how to apply those pounds of pressure to the trigger without moving the gun - at all.

That's where "press" comes into play. The fastest way to improve your shooting accuracy is to learn how to smoothly press the trigger without moving the gun. You also need to learn how to press your trigger finger independent of the rest of your hand. That's because the rest of your hand is holding the gun!

You'll hear shooters talk about "jerking" the trigger. If you look up "jerk" on Dictionary.com, you'll find a reference to a "spasmodic muscular movement." Spasmodic is generally not conducive to accurate shooting!

There's no magic secret other than focus and practice. While at the range, tune everything else out except making a smooth, motionless trigger press. Don't worry about accuracy yet. When you master a smooth trigger press, you'll soon see that all your shots tend to hit right near each other. You'll have a nice grouping of holes in the target. Once you reach that point, it's easy to place that group where you want.

How to Clean and Maintain Your XD-S Like a Boss!

HOW TO TAKE IT APART

Technically, this step is called field stripping, but as this is a PG rated book, we can stick with "take it apart." The XD-S, like most other modern pistols, is designed to be partially taken apart for normal cleaning and maintenance. There is no need to completely disassemble your pistol unless something is obviously wrong with it's function. And even then, a full disassembly and inspection is best left to a qualified gunsmith.

When you've field stripped your XD-S, you will be left with five major assemblies:

- Magazine

- Frame

- Slide

- Barrel

- Recoil spring

That's it. All necessary cleaning and lubrication can be done with this level of takedown.

BEFORE YOU BEGIN

Even before step 1 of the field stripping process, you need to make sure that your pistol is empty. Remove the magazine completely. Most importantly, rack the slide multiple times to remove the cartridge in the chamber. Now visually check the chamber. Now do it again. Lock the slide open by pressing upward on the slide lock lever while retracting the slide. When you look through the top, can you see daylight through the magazine well? Can you see that there is no cartridge in the chamber? Good. Now you're ready to proceed. Even though you are maintaining your gun, and not shooting it, always abide by the four safety rules. If you don't know them by heart, you'll find a chapter outlining them at the end of this book. OK, let's get started!

Step 1: Lock the slide open

Remember, the magazine should already be removed since you unloaded the gun. The slide should also be retracted and locked in the open position. If it's not, push upwards on the slide lock lever while retracting the slide all the way to the rear. The slide lock lever will engage the slide and prevent the recoil spring from moving it forward.

While pressing the slide lock lever up, move the slide all the way to the rear until it catches in the open position.

Your XD-S should now look like this.

Step 2: Rotate the disassembly lever

The disassembly lever is the fatter one on the left side of your XD-S, closest to the muzzle, or fiery end of the gun. If you push upwards on the front part of this lever, it will rotate in a clockwise direction to the 12 o'clock position. When done right, the disassembly lever will be oriented straight up and down. If the lever won't turn, perhaps you forgot to remove the magazine? Got it?

Rotate the disassembly lever clockwise until it's vertical.

Step 3: Unlock the slide

Here's where things start to get just a little bit tricky. Pull the slide backwards and press down on the slide release lever to disengage the slide. Allow the slide to gently move forward until it stops.

Step 4: Remove the slide

Point the gun in a safe direction, at a safe backstop, and pull the trigger. This will release the slide so it will come right off the front of your pistol.

After you pull the trigger, the slide will ease right off.

Step 5: Remove the recoil spring

The **XD-S** uses a captive recoil spring, so you don't have to worry about it flying across the room when removing. Just grab the spring by the sides and lift up as shown in the photo.

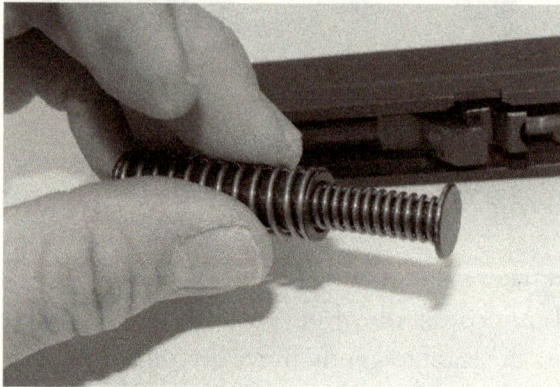

Lift the end toward the rear and pull backward out of the frame housing.

Step 6: Remove the barrel

With the recoil spring removed, you can just lift out the barrel, moving it a little bit to the rear so the muzzle comes out of the frame.

The barrel will now practically fall out. Lift the breech end and pull towards the rear.

All done!

One thing to note is that the trigger will stay in the rearward position. Leave it as is. If you mess with the trigger position, the slide will not want to go back on when you're done cleaning.

HOW TO CLEAN THE PARTS

Supplies you need

First you're going to need some basic supplies. The Springfield Armory XD-S includes a cleaning brush, but that's about it. You'll need to get a cleaning, lubricant and protectant solution, some gun cleaning patches, a cleaning rag and a brush.

There are more magic gun cleaning solvents on the market than Barney Frank's nasal hairs, but don't let that discourage you. It's pretty hard to go too wrong with any gun-specific cleaners and oils. Notice we say gun-specific. What you don't want to do is use a general purpose penetrating oil like WD-40. We love WD-40 and it's wonderful for many things, like getting bubble gum out of your hair. You may even use it to clean gun parts. Just don't rely on it as a preservative and protectant for post-cleaning use. Guns tend to get really hot, hence the need for special oil and lubricant formulations that are designed to stand up to intense heat. Heck, you can even use motor oil to lubricate guns, so they're not all that picky as long as you use something suited for the hot and dirty environment of gun guts.

Just be aware that gun oils and cleaners are not all the same. Some are designed specifically for cold conditions. Others are designed to operate dry so they don't attract fine sand into the guns' actions. Others are designed to clean only and not protect. Some are specifically designed to remove lead residue, others copper residue, others plastic residue from shotgun shells. The labels are very clear about this, so read carefully and experiment to your heart's content. You're not very likely to hurt anything. There is one caveat (or course!) and that is that the Springfield Armory XD-S features a polymer frame construction, so check to make sure your solvent is safe to use with polymer.

Once you've chosen your cleaner and lubricant - and sometimes they are in the same bottle - you'll need a couple of high tech tools and disposables to actually clean the gun.

INSANELY PRACTICAL TIP!

Budget Gun Cleaning Mat

Get yourself a scrap of indoor-outdoor carpet for a cleaning pad. It's cheap as dirt, will not get all slimy with cleaning solutions and oil and does a great job of keeping small parts from rolling off the dining room table. You can find scraps for next to nothing at most home improvement stores. Your spouse will thank you.

One of my favorites is an old toothbrush. While rough on teeth, those nylon bristles aren't going to scratch gun metal or even the polymer frames on modern pistols. And they have a nice big handle so you can clean vigorously! And no, if you're having a spat with your significant other, it's **NOT OK** to use their toothbrush.

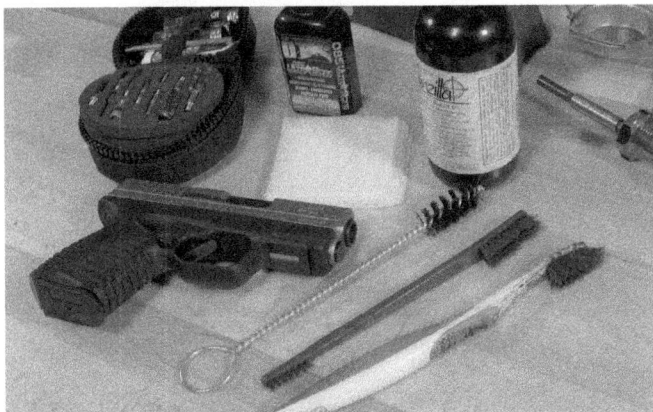

Since the XD-S comes with a bore brush, all you need is an old toothbrush and some scrap cotton.

The next thing you'll need is something to clean out the inside of the bore (the barrel.) The Springfield Armory XD-S comes with a rod with a permanent brush, which is fine for basic cleaning. Eventually, you'll want a cleaning rod or cable with a female threaded end. The end can accept an attachment that allows you to affix cloth patches for removing dirt, and cylindrical brushes for removing residue from the inside of the barrel. You can find these simple cleaning rods in kit form, complete with various size brushes and cloth patches at any gun store.

We're going to pause and put in a plug for what I believe to be the best cleaning system on the market. It's called the OTIS Technology System.

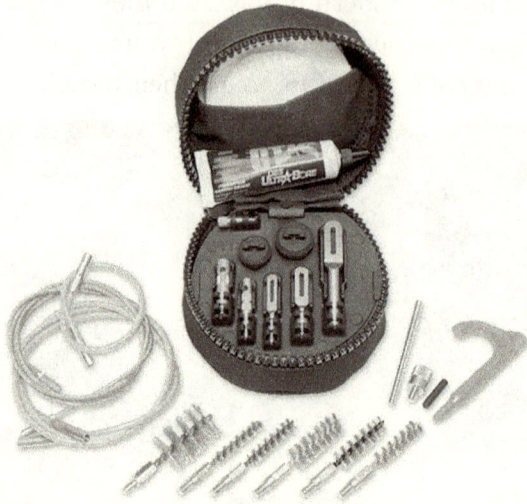

Here's the OTIS Tactical Cleaning System. The whole case is barely larger than a baseball. Image: OTIS Technology

As the story goes, the founder of OTIS, Doreen Garrett, age 16 at the time, was hunting with her Dad and got hung up on a muddy root. Doreen and her Winchester rifle pitched headlong into mud, clogging up the barrel with swamp goop. In desperation, and trying to salvage the hunt, Doreen tried to use a stick to clear the mud and the stick promptly broke, clogging up the bore even more. With hunt-less hours in the cabin to reflect on solutions to the problem, Doreen dreamed up the OTIS System. From her experience, the system had to be field-portable. But also, it was designed to clean guns from the back to the front (breech to bore) to minimize risk of damaging the crown of the barrel. The result was the design of a stiff, but flexible coated wire with various attachments for cleaning. As the "cleaning rod" was flexible, it could be rolled up into very portable field-ready kits. Now that's American ingenuity! So if you want to save yourself some trouble, consider getting an OTIS Technology System like the one shown here. It's well worth the money and the kits are designed to accommodate rifles, shotguns and pistols of various calibers. Their most basic kits will handle both 9mm and .45 ACP - all you need to clean the Springfield Armory XD-S.

When field stripped, the XD-S breaks down into these five parts and assemblies.

CLEANING THE BARREL

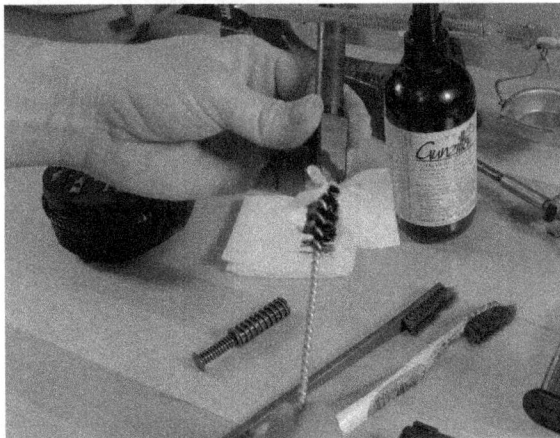

Here's a shortcut. Just put a cotton patch over the included brush, add a few drops of solvent and push it through.

Next, since your gun is field stripped, you have easy access to the barrel. Let's clean that first. Using the cleaning rod with a cleaning loop attached, stuff a cloth patch through the loop, apply some cleaner or solvent, and push (or pull) it through the barrel. Ideally do this from the breech (the back end) to the muzzle as this will pull gunk away from the action and out the muzzle.

If you haven't had the chance to get a cleaning kit yet, and are using the included brush, just stick a small cotton patch over the end as shown here, put a little bit of solvent on it, and push it all the way through the barrel from back to front. When it comes out the muzzle, just pull that patch off before drawing the brush back through.

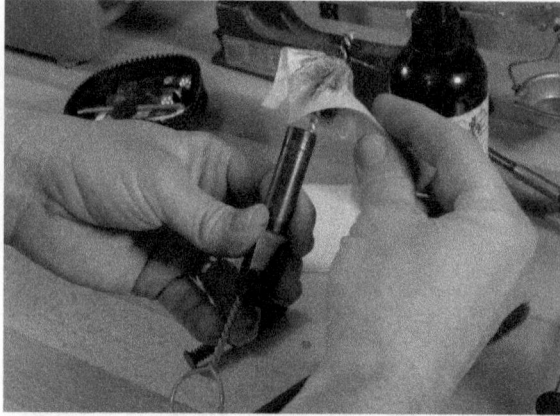

Look at all the crud that can come out with that first pass! That's why you don't start brushing right away - you don't want to scrub all that gunk around inside your barrel.

Now that you've made an initial pass through the bore with solvent and a cotton patch to get cleaner in and the loose gunk out, you can use the brush. Push or pull that through in the same direction a bunch of times.

Now it's time to brush away. Always use a nylon or brass brush as both are softer than the steel in your barrel.

Always pull or push the brush all the way through the barrel so it comes out the other end. If you try to reverse directions while the brush is in the barrel, it might get stuck and will definitely mess up your brush. The brushing will loosen stubborn stuff in the barrel like powder, lead and copper residue. The solvent you dragged through in the first step will be working to loosen dirt and mung while you do this.

Last, put your cleaning loop back on the rod and load it with a dry patch. Run that through. If it comes out dirty, put a clean patch on and repeat the process until no more dirt is coming out. Finally, check the instructions on the cleaner or lubricant you chose to see if they recommend leaving a light coat on the inside of the barrel. If you used a pure solvent or cleaner, you will need to finish the process with a fine film of lubricant or protectant.

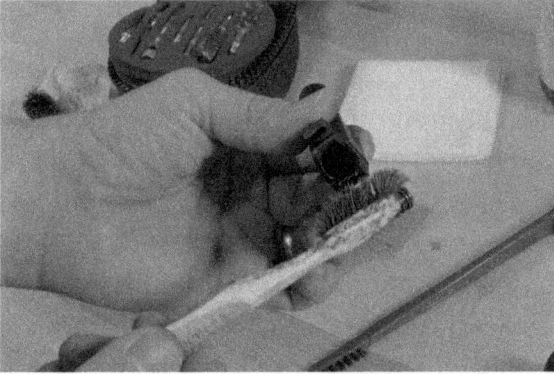

Here's where that old toothbrush comes into play. Use it to clean the outside of the barrel, the slide and frame. The toothbrush will get kind of nasty. If you want, wash it now and then with some hot water and dish soap.

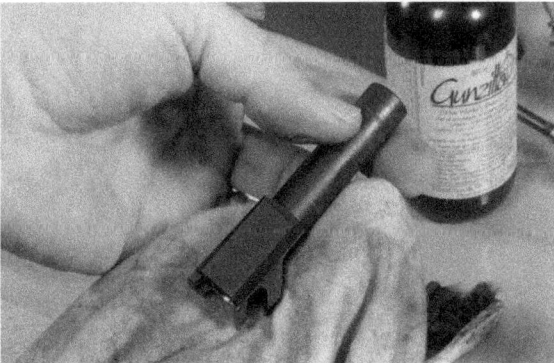

Here's a great use for that old t-shirt that doesn't fit you any more!

Now that you've cleaned the inside of the bore, clean the outside of the barrel - especially the breech (back) area as that tends to collect lots of ick. Scrub it with a toothbrush, then use an old t-shirt or cotton rag to wipe the loose dirt off.

CLEANING THE FRAME AND SLIDE

Now you get to look for dirt on the rest of the gun. Be careful not to go crazy with that cleaning toothbrush as there are small parts and springs, like slide lock levers, that can get knocked off with vigorous cleaning. Use a little cleaner, scrub with a brush, then wipe away dirt with a cloth cleaning patch or rag.

When cleaning my XD-S pistols, I like to do the following after cleaning the barrel:

Use a toothbrush to lightly scrub the breech face. This is the flat section that butts up against the cartridge, where the firing pin comes through. It will collect a little bit of crud with frequent shooting and you always want that part clean so your slide will lock into a proper fit with the barrel. It's also important to keep the breech face dry. The firing pin comes through a small hole there and you want the firing pin and channel to stay dry. If lots of oil gets in there it can jam up the motion of the firing pin, causing failures to fire.

A toothbrush is just fine for cleaning the rail lugs on the frame and the feed ramp.

Use a toothbrush to scrub the rail lugs on the frame itself. The Springfield Armory XD-S has two frame lugs on each side - one set at the very back and the other just above the takedown lever. You want both areas clean and dry for now. We'll talk about how to properly lubricate the slide and lugs in just a bit.

This is a great time to scrub the metal feed ramp in the frame itself. Just above the trigger, you'll see a small concave area that helps direct cartridges from the magazine into the barrel chamber. When you got your XD-S it was bright and shiny. Now it's likely covered with soot. Scrub that area with your brush and wipe clean and dry with a rag.

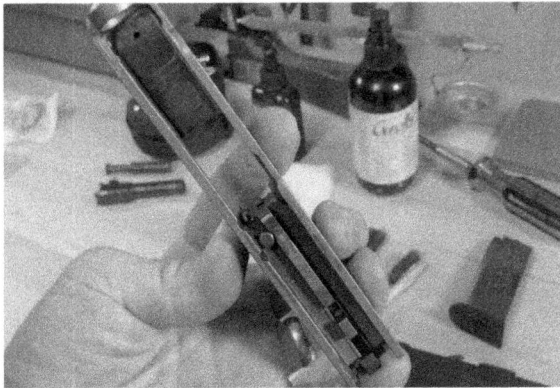

You'll need to clean the inside of the slide - there's usually a light coating of grey dusty gunk all over the interior.

You'll also want to gently clean the ejector and trigger bar with your lightly oiled rag. Use a toothbrush if you need to, just remember to keep things fairly dry, or at least dry these areas after cleaning.

The last thing to clean on the gun frame is the dust cover channel in the front of the frame. This is the half pipe shaped area under where the barrel sits. Just wipe that out with your rag - it most likely will not be all that dirty.

Now we're going to move to the steel slide itself. Use your toothbrush to scrub the long rail grooves that run the length of the slide on both sides.

Scrub the entire inside of the slide with your brush. Don't use a lot of oil or solvent as you don't want excess to ooze into the firing pin channel area.

This is an area where an actual gun cleaning brush comes in really handy as most of them have a large brush on one end and a very narrow brush on the other. The narrow brush does a great job of getting into the grooved areas.

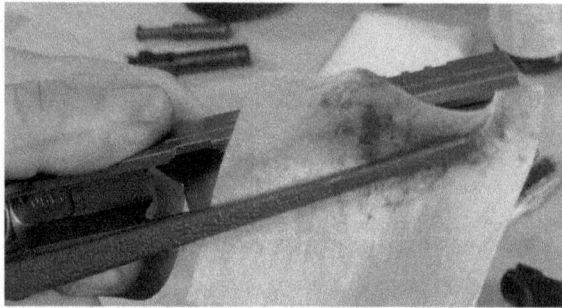

Brushes also make a great patch pusher.

After you loosen the dirt with a cleaning brush, use the small end of the cleaning brush to push a cleaning patch through the grooved areas. This really helps to remove the dirt and crud rather than just move it around.

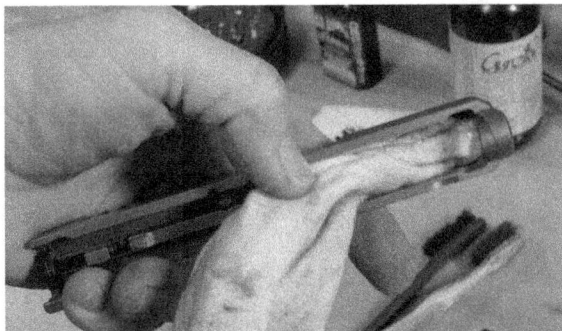

You can also stuff a portion of your cleaning rag into the front area of the slide to remove any loose dirt there.

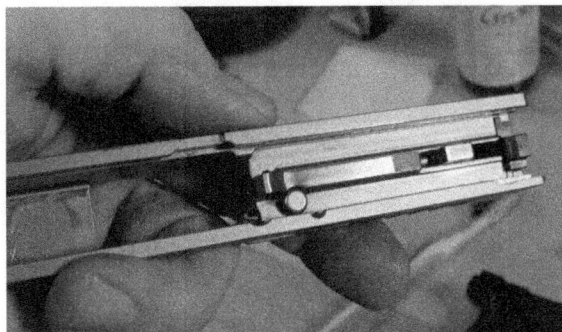

Squeaky clean and dry!

Wipe any loose dirt or oil off the recoil spring assembly. The Springfield Armory XD-S uses a captive two spring recoil system. This is fancy talk for two springs instead of one. The captive part means that when you take your XD-S apart, you don't have to worry about the main spring flying across the room!

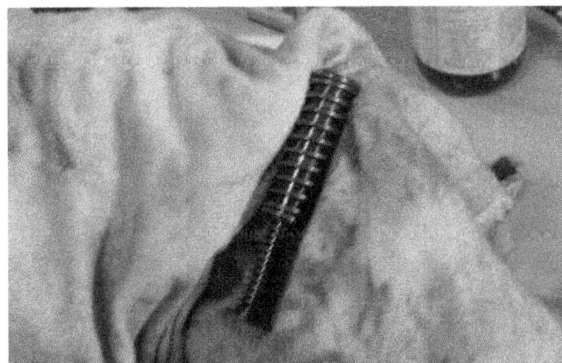

You know these photos are taken from a legit gun cleaning given the gnarly condition of this old shirt!

You don't want to soak this in oil or anything, just use a lightly oiled rag, like an old t-shirt, to wipe off loose dirt if there is any. Make sure there isn't any crud on either flat end that could impact the fit with the slide or notch in the barrel.

Clean the magazine well just like those old cartoons where someone puts a towel in one ear and pulls it out the other.

Wipe out the interior of the magazine well to make sure it's clean and dry. I like to take my cleaning rag and poke one end through the bottom of the magazine well and pull it out the top. Just be gentle as the rag will pass by the magazine latch, trigger bar and ejector as it comes out the top. These parts don't tend to get bent or pulled out easily on the XD-S, but just be aware of them as you clean. This normally does a fine job of getting any loose dirt or powder grime out of the magazine well. This is another area that requires no oil or lubrication.

Modern guns like the Springfield Armory XD-S are engineered to really take a beating and it's unlikely that you'll do it any harm by cleaning. Relax, be safe and scrub away!

LUBRICATION

The last step is to apply small amounts of lubricant. Remember, less is more with almost any gun, including the Springfield Armory XD-S. It's built to run like a champ with just a few drops of lubricant in just the right places. The more oil you slather around, the more likely it is to attract dirt, so lubricate sparingly. You can even decrease the reliability of your XD-S by using too much oil!

Lubricate your XD-S while it's still completely disassembled from cleaning. Here's how I do it on the Springfield Armory XD-S:

First, put a drop of oil on the top exterior of the barrel chamber. You can rub that drop over to the side of the chamber where the serial number and caliber of your XD-S is stamped and the side that contacts the inside of the slide.

One drop here will do the job for the chamber area.

While you're working on the barrel, put one more drop on top of the barrel right at the muzzle, about ¼ inch from the end. Rub this around the barrel a bit to smooth it out. The barrel will move back and forth through the hole in the front of the slide and you want to minimize friction and wear here.

Here I'm putting a single drop of oil in the long slide rail channel and letting it run towards the muzzle. Flip the slide over the other way and put a drop in the other channel also.

Now you want to lubricate the grooves in the slide. Put one drop in each of the interior slide channels so the oil runs down those grooves towards the muzzle. Be careful not to get oil anywhere near the firing pin channel in the rear center of the slide.

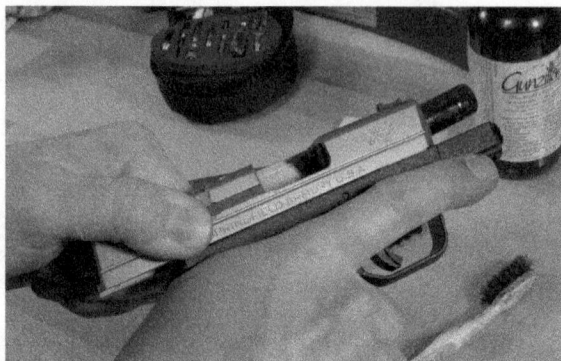

Be sure to work the slide on your XD-S after cleaning to make sure everything is put together properly!

Now, following the instructions in the next section, put your XD-S back together. Before loading a magazine, rack the slide several times (always pointing at a safe backstop) to help spread those few drops of lubricant around. If any leaks out on to the outside of your gun, just wipe it off with your cleaning rag.

REASSEMBLING YOUR SPRINGFIELD ARMORY XD-S

Putting things back together is almost the exact reverse process of taking the gun apart, but let's quickly go through that. After all, you want things to work properly right?

Step 1: Insert the barrel into the slide

Turn the slide upside down so the big open part is facing upwards. Drop the barrel in, working the muzzle of the barrel through the hole in the front of the slide. The chamber part of the barrel will drop right into place in the ejection cutout of the slide. Push the barrel towards the back of the slide (towards the rear sight) to make sure the barrel is seated properly in the slide.

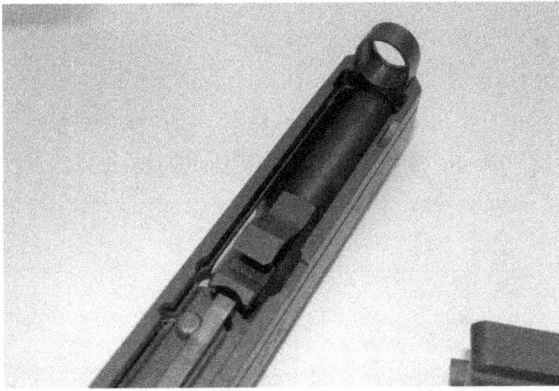

When correctly seated, the barrel will look like this in the slide.

Step 2: Install the recoil spring assembly

The XD-S uses a captive two-spring system. The larger, exterior spring goes towards the front of the gun. You'll see a cap on the end of the slide assembly that fits into a hole in the front of the slide. Push the recoil spring assembly all the way forward. Now, you'll have to squeeze the two ends of the spring assembly just a little for the rear spring cap to drop into place. There's a tiny ledge in the bottom of the barrel that will catch the rear of the recoil spring. If everything is right, the slide, barrel and recoil spring assembly will be parallel to each other.

See how the spring snaps into place?

Step 3: Install the slide

Push the slide onto the frame from the front of the gun. If anything binds or catches, check to make sure that the barrel and recoil spring are installed properly. The slide should go on very easily until you start to feel spring pressure. Push the slide all the way back and push up on the slide lock lever. Lock the slide in place to the rear.

Be sure the slide grooves fit over the rail lugs on the frame.

Step 4: Rotate the disassembly lever

Push the top of the disassembly lever forward and downward in a counter-clockwise direction until it snaps into place in a horizontal position.

With the slide locked back, rotate the disassembly lever counter-clockwise until it's horizontal again.

Step 5: Rack the slide.

Release the slide by pressing the slide lock lever or pulling the slide back and letting it go. Now rack it a few times to make sure you reassembled everything correctly.

CLEANING YOUR MAGAZINES!

Over time, dirt and dust bunnies tend to get in there. Remember, your XD-S and magazines are tools. When practicing, you'll want to eject empty magazines, let them fall on the ground (if your range allows) and reload a full magazine. When you do this, the magazines will tend to accumulate dirt, dust and maybe even mud. That's OK as long as you clean them!

But first, you have to disassemble the magazines. This is really, really easy. Here's how to do it.

Step 1: Remove the bullets

Yeah, I know, that may sound obvious, but I'm just being practical here.

Empty magazines are much easier to clean!

Step 2: Remove the base

There is a small, round locking lug right in the center of the magazine base. Ideally, use a punch to press this in. If you don't have a punch, you can use just about anything small enough to press that pin inwards - like a key or nail. Be careful not to scrape up the plastic base though.

Depress that little floor plate nub far enough for the base plate to slide forward when it unlocks.

As you remove the magazine base plate, remember that there is a big spring inside just waiting to spring and launch stuff halfway across the room, so be ready to catch it.

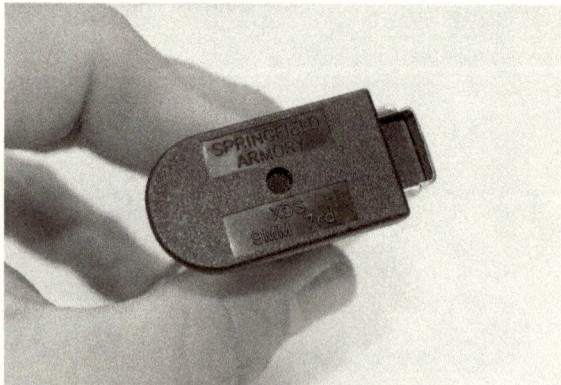

When you depress that little round button far enough, the magazine base will slide forward.

Gently allow the spring, floor plate and follower to ease out of the magazine housing. Pay close attention to the orientation of things here. Look how the floor plate is placed on the bottom of the spring. Note which way the spring itself is oriented to the magazine body. Note how the follower goes into the magazine body.

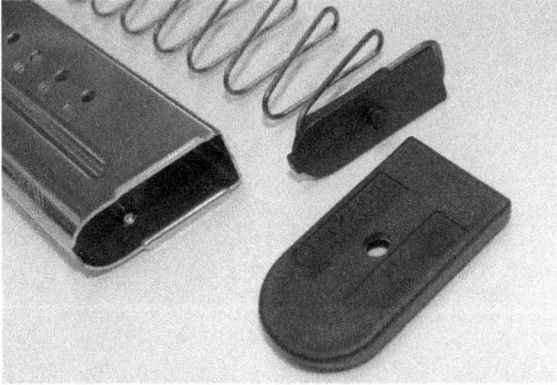

Left to right: Magazine body, magazine spring, magazine floor plate, magazine base.

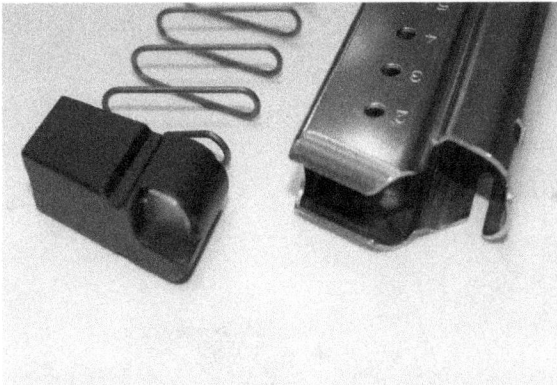

Left to right: Magazine follower, spring and magazine body.

There is a metal magazine follower plate in the plastic follower itself. This will not likely fall out on its own, nor do you really need to remove it, unless your magazine parts are really, really, really dirty.

Once you have the magazine disassembled, wipe down all parts with a clean and dry rag - like an old t-shirt. Run that rag through the magazine body itself to make sure there is no crud on the inside. You want the follower to be able to travel freely up and down inside the body.

There is no need to lubricate any of the parts in the magazine. In fact, you want to avoid that as oil does not mix well with bullets. Just get all the loose dirt and crud out of there and reassemble.

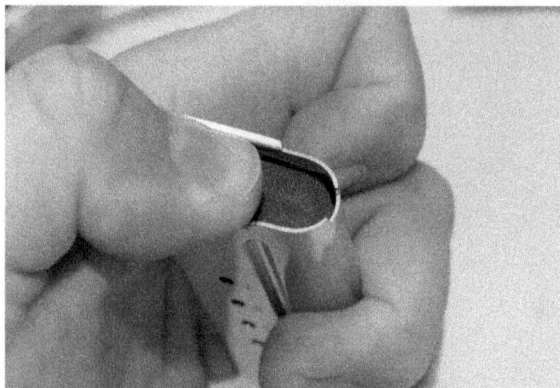

You'll need to compress the floor plate, spring and follower in order to slide the magazine base back into position.

The reassembly part is the reverse of takedown. Put the follower in, followed by the spring and magazine floor plate. Compress the spring and slide the magazine base into position until it locks into place. Right around now, you'll be glad you paid attention to exactly how everything came out!

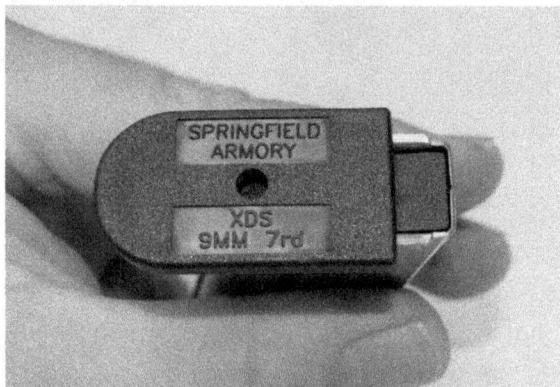

Slide the base on front to back until that button locks into place again.

FUNCTION TESTING YOUR GUN

Function testing sounds like a word space shuttle engineers would use doesn't it? All this means to to try the basic operations of your gun, before reloading it, to make sure you put it back together correctly. If there are no parts left over on the table, you're off to a great start!

When you're finished cleaning, using all dry-fire precautions listed below, test your gun to be sure you put things back together correctly.

1. Remove the magazine.

2. Rack the slide and visually verify that the chamber is empty.

3. Rack the slide, point at a safe backstop, and press the trigger. Everything sound OK? Good. Now repeat the process to be sure before loading or securing your XD-S.

Some people like to clean their gun at the range when they are finished shooting. This way, after reassembly, they can fire a couple of test shots to make sure the gun is put back together in working order. That's another benefit of using one of the portable OTIS Technology kits. You can bring everything you need with you without filling your shooting bag with loose cleaning supplies.

Accessorizing Your XD-S

Even though the Springfield Armory XD-S is a pocket-sized pistol, there are a number of ways to accessorize it to fit your preferences and anticipated uses of your gun.

The Springfield Armory XD-S includes a single slot picatinny rail so you can mount lasers, lights or even a bayonet if you're expecting zombies.

LASERS

Lasers? On a pocket pistol like the Springfield Armory XD-S? Absolutely!

If you choose to carry a Springfield Armory XD-S for personal protection, addition of a laser can make a dramatic difference in your ability to put shots on target quickly and accurately in low-light conditions. In a high-stress situation, you need to be looking for threats - and when you find one, you need to get your gun on target quickly. Lasers allow you to accomplish two things:

1. Effectively aim your gun while your eyes are focused on the threat.

2. Effectively aim your gun from non-traditional firing positions.

After shooting several events and training classes in low-light and no-light conditions, I came to an understanding of exactly what this means. When looking for threats, your eyes are focused exactly on that - potential threats around you. They're not naturally focused on your front sight. If your gun is raised into a proper shooting position, where your eyes are lined up with the sights, the gun is obstructing much of your forward view as you look - because it's right in front of your face! Use of a laser, with practice, allows you to aim and shoot, even while your gun is below a normal sighting position.

Do lasers make you a better shot? Not directly. Are they a replacement for standard sights? Nope. They are a tool that provides more sighting options, especially in lower light conditions. If you ever get a chance to take a training class with at least some low-light training scenarios, take it. I guarantee it will be an enlightening experience!

Crimson Trace LG-469 Laserguard

The Laserguard is a nifty upgrade to your Springfield Armory XD-S. The Laserguard mounts in front of the trigger guard so it does not add any length or width to your XD-S. Since the width of the Laserguard is less than the width of the XD-S slide, your gun is still just as thin as it was before installation.

Not only does it match the color of your XD-S, the Crimson Trace Laserguard adds hardly any bulk.

Like most other Crimson Trace products, the Laserguard features Instinctive Activation. A pressure pad is on the front of the grip, so when you grasp the XD-S in a normal firing grip, the laser is activated automatically. With a bit of practice, you can vary the pressure of your middle finger in order to turn the laser on and off.

While no appreciable weight or bulk is added to the gun with installation of the Laserguard, you will need a holster designed for it. Fortunately there are plenty of options available. See the Holsters chapter for a few ideas.

The Crimson Trace Laserguard for the XD-S will run continuously for about four hours, which is a long time when you think about it. It only activates when you squeeze the grip so it doesn't stay on for extended periods of time. It's pre-sighted at the factory, but you can easily adjust windage (side to side) and elevation (up and down) with an included tool.

LaserMax Micro

You've heard the phrase "apples and oranges" right? Essentially it means both are good, just different. It's the same with laser designs. While Crimson Trace believes in *Instinctive Activation*, where the laser comes on automatically, LaserMax believes in *Controlled Activation*, where the user determines when the laser should be on and off.

The LaserMax Micro is small enough to fit most any rail-equipped pistol.

Which one is right? Neither. Or maybe both. It's a personal preference issue - like boxers vs. briefs or pumps vs. flats. I've shot both in training environments and each has pros and cons. The decision boils down to which you prefer for your specific needs. Do you want the manual control or do you not want to think about having to activate your laser?

The LaserMax UNI-MAX Micro is a teensy tiny thing. It will mount on most any pistol with a rail, and it works especially well with the Springfield Armory XD-S.

The LaserMax Micro activation levers are easily accessible on both sides of the unit.

The size of the XD-S lends itself to a good partnership with the LaserMax Micro. The activation paddles are on both sides of the laser body and you can easily reach them with an extended trigger finger. Operation is identical from either side, so the unit is ready to go for righties or lefties.

The battery will run for about five hours and you can switch between constant and pulse modes at any time. You'll need a compatible holster, but plenty are available.

SIGHT UPGRADES

The factory sights on the Springfield Armory XD-S are perfectly serviceable in daylight conditions. The fiber optic front sight, with its green or red tube, is easy to see and works effectively even in lower light conditions.

However, if you intend to use your Springfield Armory XD-S as a concealed carry or home defense pistol, you may want to consider upgrading the factory sights to glow-in-the-dark night sights.

TruGlo TFO Tritium Fiber Optic

The idea behind the TFO sights is to combine fiber optic tubes with tritium power sources. This accomplishes two things:

1. Provide outstanding visibility in daylight conditions. The brighter it is outside, the more your sights jump out at you. The fiber optic tubes are just about ½ inch long. The tube collects available light from the top and concentrates it at the base of the tube, thereby creating a really, really bright dot sight.

2. Provide outstanding visibility in low or no light conditions. This is where the tritium comes into play. At the muzzle end of each fiber optic tube is a tritium lamp which emits light through the tube. This creates a glowing dot powered by tritium instead of light collected by the fiber optic tube.

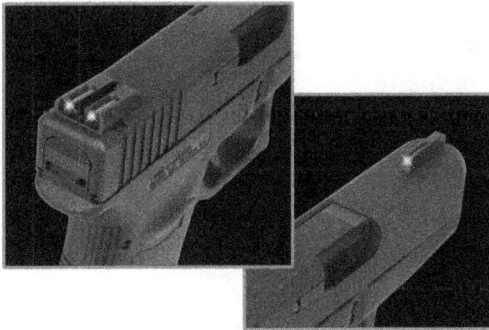

TruGlo TFO Sights are great in daylight and no light.
Image: TruGlo

TruGlo TFO sights are now available in either all green (front and back sights) or a combination of yellow and green. If you go the combination route, you'll see that the yellow sights on the rear are deliberately less bright than the green. This helps the front sight to visibly stand out from the rear sights – which is especially important in low light conditions. With a bright green dot flanked on either side by yellow dots, there is simply no way to confuse sight alignment.

The Fiber Optic tubes are enclosed on three sides by CNC machined steel frames so there is minimal risk of damage to the tubes. We should also note that the sights are closed at the muzzle end, thereby preventing anyone from seeing the glow – day or night.

XS Big Dot Sights

XS Sights take a different approach to traditional handgun sighting configurations. Rather than a one dot in front, two in the back or notch and post configuration, the XS flagship handgun sight offerings is the Express Big Dot. And it's exactly that. The front sight is replaced by a large circular sight. The center is a green tritium glow in the dark dot. That's surrounded by a large white ring. So the big dot out front is designed to be super easy to see in both day and night conditions. Rather than more dots on the back, the rear sight is a shallow "v" with a vertical stripe in the center. To aim the XS Big Dot setup, just dot the "i" by placing the huge front sight on top of the vertical line on the rear sight. Couldn't be easier.

The big benefit of the XS Big Dot sights on a gun like the Springfield Armory XD-S is speed. When you raise the gun to eye level, you can't help but see that huge, round front sight - immediately. It's fast and plenty accurate.

Don't let anyone mislead you here. Some folks whimper that the XS Big Dot sights are not precise enough for accuracy shooting. Bull hockey. With XS Big Dot sights you can hit targets at any reasonable distance for the the Springfield Armory XD-S. I can just about guarantee that the combination of the Springfield Armory XD-S and XS Big Dot Sights will be more accurate than the average shooters ability.

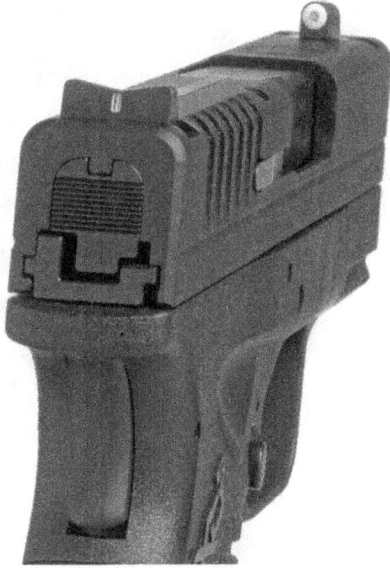

XS Big Dot Sights. Image: XS Sights.

OTHER UPGRADES

Pearce Magazine Extension

Here's a way that ten bucks can make a huge difference.

As we discussed earlier in the book, Springfield Armory offers a larger capacity magazine that adds two rounds and more gripping area to the Springfield Armory XD-S. With the extended magazine in place, you'll be able to get three fingers on the grip. These extended magazines are great and I highly recommend that you buy some. But the extra round capacity comes at a price - increased size. The extended magazine will add about ⅞ of an inch to the height of your gun. And this extra height makes concealment just a tad more difficult.

Pearce magazine extensions add a bit more grip space for your pinky. Image: Pearce

The Pearce Grip Extension helps you compromise. You simply slide the magazine extension on to your standard magazine in place of the existing magazine floor plate. See the cleaning chapter to see how to take apart your magazine. Once in place, the Pearce Magazine Extension allows most people to get a third finger on the front of the grip. As it's an angled design, there is no "height" added to the rear of your grip, so it's a bit easier to conceal than the Springfield Armory extended capacity magazine. Of course, this type of extension only gives you more gripping surface - it does not add any capacity to your magazine.

Spare Magazines

Here's where I get on the soapbox and implore you to buy more magazines for your XD-S - now, while it's brand new! Load up. Buy four or five.

Here's why.

Guns require magazines! A gun without magazines is like a Justin Bieber concert without screaming twelve year olds. Your Springfield Armory XD-S will last a couple of lifetimes with some basic care, and down the road, magazines won't be as easy to come by, or as affordable. The other more practical consideration is that you'll want at least five magazines should you take any sort of training class. You'll also need at least five magazines if you get adventurous and shoot your XD-S in a local competition, like an IPDA match. Last, but not least, it's nice to have a pile of magazines when you go to practice at the range - you can spend more time shooting and less time reloading magazines.

> *Everyone should carry at least one spare magazine. This is very important in a relatively low-capacity pistol like the XD-S. But it's also important because many pistol malfunctions can be traced to the magazine, and you may need to replace a malfunctioning magazine in the middle of a fight. And anyway, should you have the great misfortune to get in a gunfight, as the late Col. Jeff Cooper noted, "it's poor form to go home with an empty pistol."*
>
> Mike Barham, Media and Public Relations Manager, Galco Gunleather

For all the above reasons, just trust me on this and stock up on magazines now. Like that 401K plan, it's hurts a bit now, but you'll be thankful later.

10 Ways To Carry Your Springfield Armory XD-S: Holster Options

"At Galco, we recommend building a "holster wardrobe" to take advantage of the many concealment options a pistol like the XD-S offers. Just as you need multiple pairs of shoes for hiking, church, and the gym, you need different holsters to allow you to carry your favored pistol all the time. This might take the form of, for example, an IWB, an ankle holster, and a pocket holster to accommodate different types of clothing and perhaps different situations. Yes, it costs more, but refer back to the First Rule of Gunfighting - always have a gun! And numerous holster options helps you to avoid rationalizing carrying a less effective pistol like a tiny .380 when you can and should carry a 9mm or .45 if at all possible."

Mike Barham, Media and Public Relations Manager, Galco Gunleather

The Springfield Armory XD-S is a very small, and very portable handgun. As tempting as it is, never, ever, ever carry it in a pocket (or anywhere else) without a proper holster.

Why?

Holsters serve three primary purposes:

1. **Make your gun safely accessible.** If you ever need to access your gun under stress, it needs to be exactly where you expect it, oriented in the specific way that you expect and easily extractable from wherever you keep it. If you treat your gun like that six month old roll of Wintergreen Certs, you never know where it will be. Buried in your pocket amongst change and movie ticket stubs?

Under a cell phone, set of keys and garage door opener in your purse? In your backpack or briefcase under 7 weeks of late expense report receipts? A good holster keeps your gun in a specific position, 100% of the time, all the time, every time. Yes, that's redundant. Yes, that's redundant. See what I did there?

2. **Keep your gun secure.** I said "your gun" for a reason. That reason is that it is, your gun, and should always be, your gun. It shouldn't become someone else's gun when you jump out of your Barcolounger suddenly and decide to spackle the garage. It should also stay put when that special someone decides to teach you the Cupid Shuffle at that slightly-awkward office party. In short, a good holster will keep your gun exactly where it should be, under your control, through the range of your daily physical activities.

3. **Prevent someone or something from discharging the gun.** A good holster helps protect the trigger of your gun - from you and your stuff. When you go to retrieve your gun from any type of holster - pocket, belt, ankle or other - your fingers get all grabby by necessity. Part of the holsters job is to cover the trigger while your thumb and fingers find and assume a proper grip on your handgun. Only after you have assumed a proper and safe grip should the gun come out of the holster. A good holster also protect your trigger from stuff. Strange as it sounds, there are far too many documented cases of negligent discharges resulting from some other item in a pocket or purse working its way into the trigger area. External items can even apply pressure through clothing to activate a trigger. Rare, but possible. Life's too short to walk around with an unprotected trigger.

GALCO TUCK-N-GO AND GALCO STOW-N-GO INSIDE THE PANT HOLSTERS

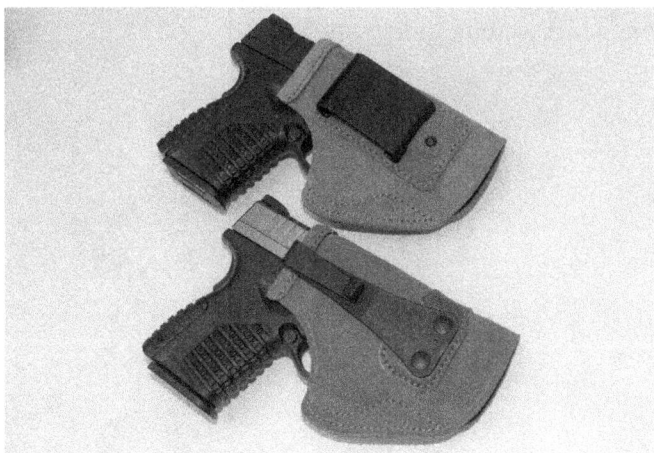

The Stow-N-Go (top) and Tuck-N-Go (bottom) are both part of the Galco Carry Lite series.

Both holsters are intended for simple, deep concealment. They feature an open-top design for quick access, a reinforced mouth for one-handed reholstering and open bottoms to let dirt fall out. Both have a vertical orientation which allows for different carry options. You can use them behind the hip bone or in an appendix position. In case you don't know, "appendix carry" simply means mounting your holster on your belt just in front of where your appendix might be. Of course, if you're a lefty, estimate on the opposite side. The exterior of the leather is a bit rough to help keep the holster in place via friction with your clothes.

The difference is that the Tuck-N-Go is, well, tuckable! The plastic clip goes over your belt with most of it hidden behind the belt itself. A small "J" clip hooks onto the bottom of the belt and is barely visible. The whole clip assembly is only attached at the bottom to the holster, which allows you to tuck a shirt or blouse over the gun and between the holster and clip. With a compact gun like the Springfield Armory XD-S it's a great solution for environments where you have to dress up a bit, yet keep your gun fully concealed.

The Stow-N-Go has a wide belt clip with a hook on the bottom to keep the holster in place while you draw. It's not a tuckable model, so you will have to use some type of cover garment like a jacket or untucked shirt to fully hide your XD-S.

Notice the "rough side out" leather. This helps keep the holster, and your gun, in place.

RECLUSE POCKET HOLSTER

The Springfield Armory XD-S is small enough to be a pocket gun. For all practical purposes, it's even a tad smaller than a snub-nosed revolver like the Ruger LCR.

While the XD-S is small enough to dump in your pocket, never, ever, ever do so without using a pocket holster. A pocket holster addresses all three criteria addressed at the beginning of this chapter, but especially the safety part. If you carry a gun in your pocket, you need to make sure the trigger is properly protected.

There are lots of pocket holsters on the market, but what I really like about the Recluse design is that it **completely** hides the profile of your gun. I mean completely.

The large, flat and smooth front panel prevents any outline of the XD-S from "printing" through the fabric of your pocket. While someone looking closely may see that you have something in your pocket, there is no hint as to what that something is.

Recluse Holsters feature a large front panel which completely hides the profile of your XD-S.

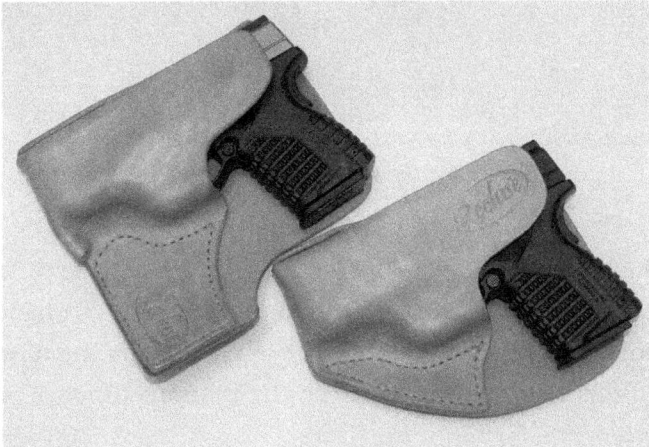

The Recluse Holster Model on the left is designed for larger cargo pockets. The wide base prevents the weight of the gun from tipping the holster in your pocket.

All of the leather in the Recluse holster is somewhat stiff and sturdy. In addition to helping hide your gun, the structure helps keep your gun in the proper orientation in the pocket.

One other difference in the Recluse design is the "hinged" operation. Since the entire outside of the gun is covered with the leather panel, there has to be a way to get your fingers around the grip in order to draw, right? The interior leather flap is slit about ¾ of the way from top to bottom, allowing the trigger guard pocket, and your gun, to push away from the front panel. There is plenty of room to slip your fingers between the front leather panel and your gun, so you can get a proper firing grip before drawing. As I would say with any holster, be sure to practice this motion - a lot - with an unloaded gun. You want the draw motion to be completely instinctive.

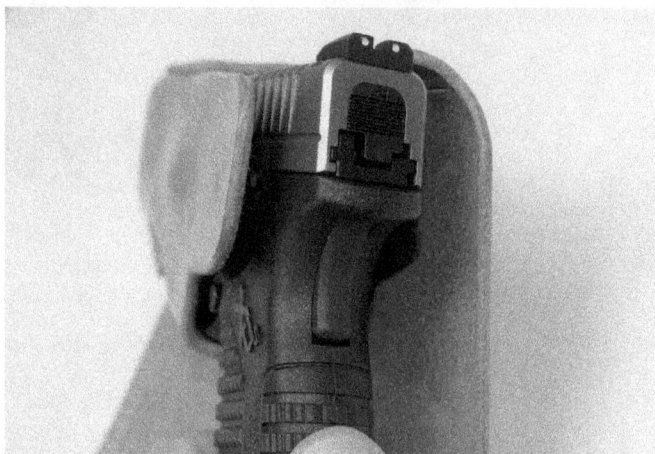

Here's the stand-out feature of Recluse Holsters - the hinge flap which hides the profile of your gun, yet still allows you to obtain a firing grip on the gun while it's holstered.

But what if you have a laser mounted on your XD-S? According to Tod Cole at Recluse, no worries. They will be offering models compatible with Crimson Trace, LaserMax and Viridian lasers. Status on availability of the Recluse, and other holsters mentioned here, can change daily, so be sure to check the manufacturers web sites for the latest offerings.

CROSSBREED SNAPSLIDE

One of the really nice things about the Springfield Armory XD-S is that it's thin and "short" enough to easily conceal using an outside the waistband holster.

For OWB carry, I particularly like the CrossBreed SnapSlide holster for a few of different reasons.

Like the IWB counterparts, the leather back and kydex holster pouch give a great combination of "thin" yet comfortable. The portion of the holster on the outside of the gun simply cannot be thinner with any other material than Kydex.

The CrossBreed SnapSlide shown here with a .45 ACP Springfield Armory XD-S with a Crimson Trace LG-469 Laserguard.

The generous leather panel and widely-spaced belt loops offer great comfort and stability with a 1 ½ inch or 1 ¼ inch gun belt. I had no problem adjusting the carry position from anywhere between 3 and 5:30 positions, assuming a right handed configuration.

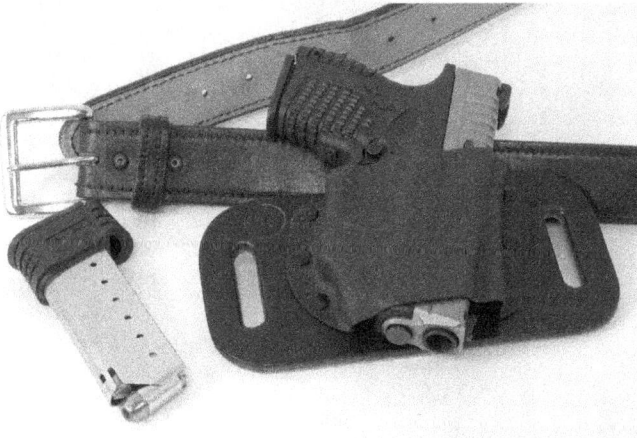

Note how high the gun rides with the CrossBreed SnapSlide holsters. Hardly anything extends below your belt.

The SnapSlide holds the XD-S high relative to the belt level which aids in concealment. This high positioning and short barrel of the

Springfield Armory XD-S mean that hardly any of the gun extends below belt level, so an untucked shirt or blouse easily covers your gun.

One more thing to note - the SnapSlide is available in a configuration compatible with the Crimson Trace LG-469 Laserguard. The three together make an outstanding concealed carry package that's light, trim and functional.

GALCO ANKLE LITE

While I don't recommend ankle holsters for your primary carry method, unless you have to, the XD-S makes a great ankle gun. Whether it's your primary gun or a backup gun, the XD-S lends itself to comfortable ankle carry.

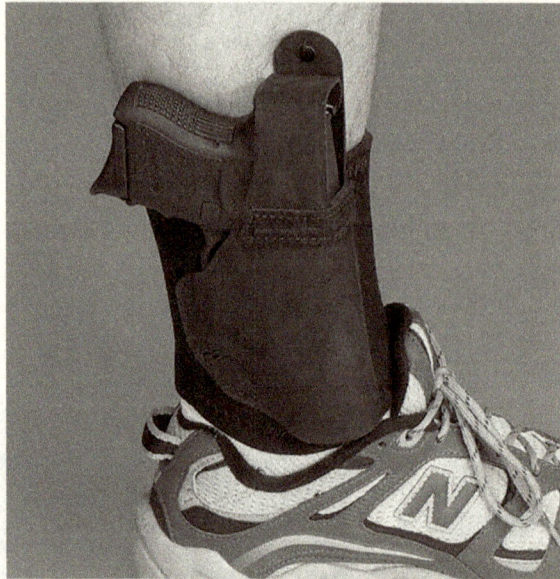

The cushy neoprene band is comfortable, yet durable.

Although the XD-S itself is pretty light, a full magazine of 9mm or .45 ACP ammo adds weight, so you want a comfortable ankle holster. The Galco Ankle Lite uses a wide, and thick, neoprene band for support. Neoprene is that squishy but strong stuff used to make wetsuits. Obviously this provides a built-in advantage against sweat as well.

If you do a lot of physical activity throughout your day, order the optional calf-strap to prevent the holster and gun from slipping down when you run and jump.

N82 TACTICAL

In case N82 Tactical is new to you, it's pronounced "Nate Squared" Tactical. That's because a whole bunch of Nate's started up the place. More than should be legal probably, as high-capacity Nate's must be dangerous, but who I am to judge? I met them at the 2012 SHOT Show when I was finishing up The Insanely Practical Guide to Gun Holsters and got the full tour of N82 Tactical's engineering prowess.

The N82 holsters have some interesting innovations. Spurred on to entrepreneurial enterprise by the belief that holsters should be both comfortable and comforting, the dynamic Nate duo and a rental squad of Oompa Loompas created a basic design that makes for an inherently wearable, yet solid and secure inside the waistband holster.

The N82 is a multi-layer affair. A large backing panel goes between the gun and your tender midsection skin areas. The panel is large enough to completely cover the gun and all or most of the grip — depending on the specific model. This keeps sharp and abrasive stuff away from your belly. A belt clip is affixed to the gun pocket so the whole mess is tucked inside the waistband with the clip securing to your belt. Pretty simple.

Here's where the layering comes in.

The body side of the panel is made from soft suede. N82 Tactical chose suede for several reasons. It's a natural material, so it allows your skin to breathe and feel cool — even in hot and humid climates. Another reason for the suede lining is that it has a friction coefficient. Yeah, I told you we wouldn't get into quantum physics and material dynamics in this book, but hang in there for a second. Since the whole suede area has some "grip" it serves to spread the weight of the gun over a broader area. Not that we're calling your area broad or anything. OK, enough of the fancy science.

Sandwiched in the middle is a layer of neoprene. If you saw the movie Jaws, or have been to Sea World, you'll know that this is the stuff that diver's wetsuits are made of. It's waterproof. While you probably won't be diving with your N82 Tactical holster, the neoprene barrier does in fact create a moisture barrier between your sweaty broad area and your expensive gun. Even if you sweat, your gun stays dry. Within reason of course. The other reason behind the neoprene moisture barrier is to prevent the leather portion of the holster from becoming mushier and mushier over time. Three out of four Nate's believe that leather doesn't ever stop breaking in. It continues to get softer and softer over time, especially with exposure to moisture. We're not sure what doctors and dentists believe.

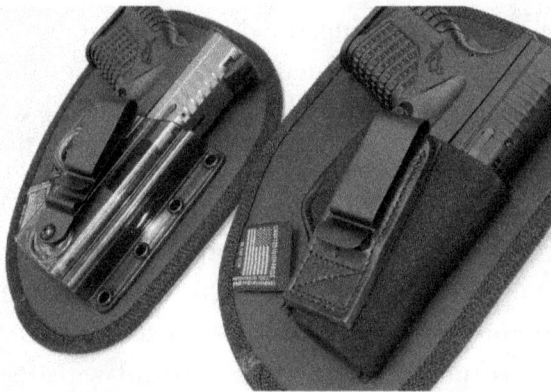

An XD-S .45 ACP in the N82 Tactical Professional (left) and XD-S 9mm in a N82 Tactical Original Tuckable (right)

The outer layer is leather. This provides structure and stability and a safe backing for your gun.

For the gun pocket itself, N82 Tactical offers a couple of separate options — the Standard and Professional Series. Here's where things get fun for carrying the Springfield Armory XD-S.

The original model, or Standard Series, utilizes a stretchy material to secure the gun to the leather holster panel. This model works like a champ with the XD-S. Better yet, if you have a laser, like the Crimson Trace LG-469 Laserguard mounted on your XD-S, it will fit into this model. It's a two-fer.

On the Professional Series models, the gun pocket is made from a polycarbonate material. Yes, the same material that is used to make impact resistant glasses, bulletproof glass and Justin Bieber CD's. The polycarbonate is molded so that it protrudes slightly into the trigger guard of the gun to provide positive retention. When wearing the holster, your body presses the gun even more into the trigger guard mold. To draw the gun, use a rotating motion along the axis of the barrel. This releases the trigger guard and allows the gun to exit the holster. It sounds complicated, but when you wear this holster just behind the hip bone, your natural draw motion tends to rotate the gun exactly as needed to release the gun. After a couple of tries I had it down pat.

We were pleasantly surprised at the engineering involved in this concealed carry holster. While it looks simple, there's a lot under the covers, so to speak.

The best part? It's ridiculously comfortable with the thin profile of the Springfield Armory XD-S.

GALCO BELLY BAND

Belly bands are infinitely flexible. You can wear it high or low, with a tucked in shirt or blouse or not. Galco makes the best one I've tried.

The Springfield Armory XD-S fits into either of the leather gun pockets.

It's made from a four inch wide elastic band with two leather gun pockets. The gun pockets are oriented on opposing angles so you can carry a gun canted forward or backward and on either side - or both - of your body. Turning the Underwraps Belly Band inside out makes it equally compatible with righties and lefties. There are two additional pouches for spare magazines or maybe handcuffs, if you're into that sort of thing.

GALCO KINGTUK

I use the Galco KingTuk almost daily for my full size 1911. Why? In my opinion, Galco has created the best "hybrid" holster on the market. There are plenty of good ones, but Galco takes the extra fit and finish steps. You'll find the leather edges perfectly finished. The Kydex edges are polished smooth. The metal clips are perfectly finished and won't snag or catch on your clothes. It's just a Cadillac implementation of the hybrid design.

The Galco King Tuk has a large (relative to the XD-S) leather backing for stability and comfort.

Galco also makes a KingTuk for the Springfield Armory XD-S. Given the super-thin design of the XD-S, this makes a very realistic tuckable holster option as there is hardly any tell tale bulge. Try this combination mounted at the 4 or 8 o'clock position depending on your right or left hand preference.

GALCO POCKET PROTECTOR HOLSTER

Galco makes a handy pocket holster for the Springfield Armory XD-S. It's a rough side out leather design, which helps keep the holster in your pocket when you draw. There is also a leather "hook" cut into the top of the stabilizing panel which is intended to catch on the inside of your pocket, making sure the holster stays put when your gun is removed.

The open top of this holster is molded to the rectangular profile of the XD-S so re-holstering is easy. I also find that the extra-sturdy leather stabilizing panel keeps a fully loaded XD-S stable in my pocket. I've had less sturdy pocket holsters that were not strong enough to hold a top-heavy gun in the upright position in my pocket.

Note the rough leather exterior and hook design. Both features help keep the holster in your pocket when the gun comes out.

Simple and effective. I use this one a lot.

GALCO PMC POCKET MAGAZINE CARRIER

I've gotten in the habit of carrying a spare magazine in my support side pants pocket. No, it's not some high-speed, low-drag tactical thing. I'm a high-drag kind of guy anyway. It's more a result of ease and convenience. Having things to conceal on both sides of my body just seems like a chore and carrying magazines on my belt spoils the one comfortable side of my body that I have left.

The problem with carrying a magazine in the pocket is that it flops around as you walk, sit and do whatever else it is that you do. If you ever need to grab it quickly, it is almost guaranteed to be in the "wrong" position. For example, when I use a belt magazine carrier, I want the spare magazines oriented with bullets facing forward when mounted on my support side. Then, when I grab a spare magazine from that location, my index finger is already lined up on the front of the magazine. Inserting it into the pistol is then smooth and effortless. When that magazine is flopping around in my pocket, it might be facing forward, backward or even upside down. I'll almost certainly have some fumbling to do to get it into my pistol.

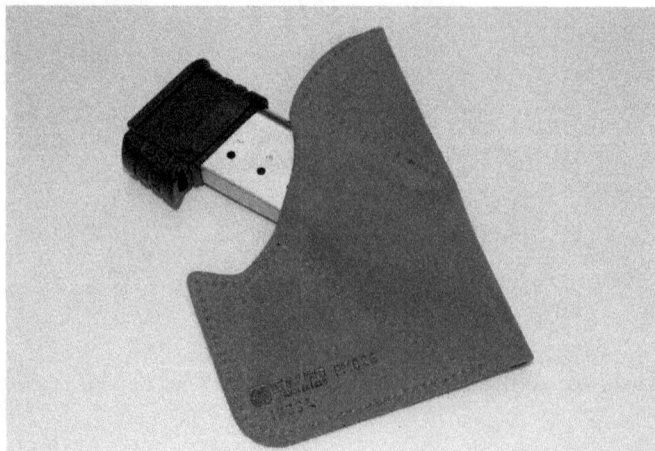

Galco designed the PMC Pocket Magazine Carrier with rigid leather to keep a loaded magazine oriented properly in your pocket. The rough exterior and "hook" design help keep it in your pocket as you remove the magazine.

The Galco PMC Pocket Magazine Carrier holds the magazine at a 45 degree angle exactly how I want it. Galco makes the carrier out of sturdy leather that is "inside out" and full pocket width. The firm leather keeps the whole thing stable inside of your pocket, while the rough outside creates a friction grip on the inside of your pocket. This helps prevent you from pulling the carrier out with the magazine. That would certainly be embarrassing in a life or death self defense situation.

This works great in pants pockets, but helps with other carry locations too. I've used it in larger cargo pants pockets and it's large enough so that it doesn't spill over sideways. You can also use it in a coat or blazer pocket. Ladies, it also makes a great purse carry accessory. Put this in an interior pocket and you'll know exactly where your spare magazine is.

GALCO UDCMC MAGAZINE CARRIER

If you want a belt-mounted magazine carrier, this one is simple and effective.

It's a slide on model, so you don't have to plan in advance to mount it on your belt. Just slip the polymer "hook" over your belt and down until the bottom hook catches the lower edge of your belt. It's pre-sized for 1 ¼" belts, but will work almost as well with thinner belts.

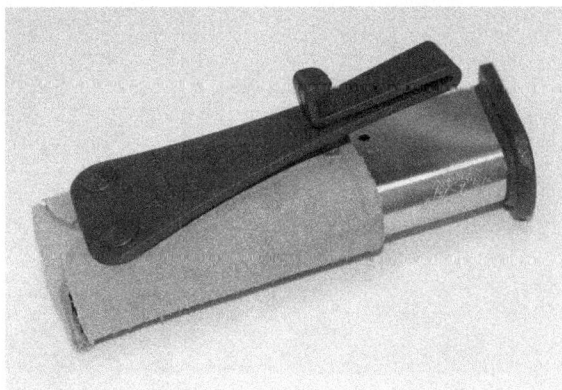

Note the hook on the belt fastener. This prevents the magazine carrier from coming up with the magazine. The gap between the mount and leather pouch allows the carrier to be fully tuckable.

The UDCMC Magazine Carrier is constructed from horsehide, with the rough side out and smooth side in. This allows the magazine to be easily inserted and extracted while the rough exterior helps keep the carrier in place with a little friction.

The best part? This model is tuckable. The polymer clip is only attached at the bottom, so once the carrier is mounted on your belt, you can tuck a shirt or blouse between the magazine carrier and your pants and belt. The clip itself is almost entirely hidden by the belt.

Neato.

GALCO MERIDIAN HOLSTER HANDBAG

Ladies, this one is specifically for you. If you choose to carry in your purse, be sure to do it safely. Don't let your XD-S flop around in a main purse compartment along with all sorts of other daily paraphernalia. That's asking for trouble. Not only will it be hard to find your gun during an emergency, you run the risk of something getting caught up in the trigger - with potentially disastrous consequences.

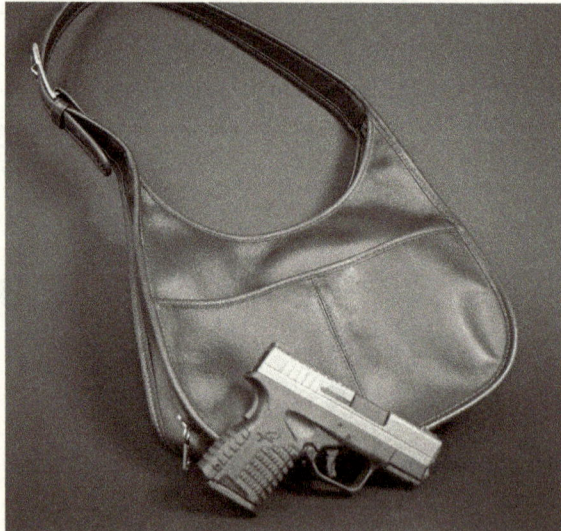

The Galco Meridian Holster Handbag is a stylish pocketbook - with a secret.

If you choose purse carry, be sure to keep your gun in a dedicated compartment. That's where a quality holster handbag like the Galco Meridian shines.

The Meridian is a fine looking and functional handbag with a magnetically closing outside compartment, main interior compartment and separate interior compartment. Most importantly, it features a dedicated gun holster compartment accessible via a lockable vertical zipper on the exterior. Inside this compartment is a sewn-in holster pouch with a Velcro retention strap which can be removed if you prefer. We found that the retention strap is unnecessary with the XD-S in this purse - the gun will stay in the holster pocket just fine.

The Galco Meridian is available in black or chocolate brown. Galco makes a variety of styles with similar concealed carry functionality. Check out more options at GalcoGunleather.com.

The dedicated holster compartment not only keeps your gun hidden - it also keeps the trigger protected while offering immediate access.

AND MORE...

I love holsters. Established companies and young upstarts are always inventing new carry solutions, so the options listed here are only intended to get you started.

If you want to learn about holsters and all the ways to carry a gun, check out my book, <u>The Insanely Practical Guide to Gun Holsters</u>. You can also subscribe to my weekly email at <u>MyGunCulture.com</u>. I'm always covering new holster options there.

Ammunition for the Springfield Armory XD-S

The performance of any gun is only as good as the ammunition you put into it. And I'm not just talking about using any quality self-defense ammunition.

One of the reasons that 9mm guns are more effective today than ever before is the performance of modern 9mm ammunition. Of course, improvements are not limited to 9mm - .45 ACP performance, at it's lower velocity, is also in a golden age.

A 9mm XD-S (center) shown here with a Springfield Armory EMP 9mm (left) and Glock 26 9mm.

Before we talk about some great ammunition options for the Springfield Armory XD-S, we need to spend a minute discussing bullet design.

Modern self-defense expanding ammunition considers opposing factors to gain the best overall performance - penetration and expansion. Both of these attributes are impacted by velocity. More velocity tends to drive expansion at a faster rate. At any given velocity, a bullet can expand less rapidly and penetrate more, or expand more rapidly and penetrate less. It's kind of like diving into a pool. If you enter the water vertically, with your hands pointed in front of you like an Olympic diver, you'll go deeper. If you jump off the board and do a spectacular belly flop, you won't go very deep, although you may wish you would quietly sink to the bottom, thereby ending your misery.

When ammunition companies design a specific round, say a 9mm, they will create a bullet that will travel a certain depth into standardized ballistic gelatin at an expected average velocity for the caliber in an "average" gun. So, as an example, ACME Road Runner Blaster 9mm ammo might be expected to fire at 1,150 feet per second from something like a Glock 17. ACME might design the bullet to penetrate somewhere in the 10 to 14 inch range while expanding fully.

Wait a minute! This is supposed to be a book about the Springfield Armory XD-S! Why all this diversion into ammunition design? Here's why. While there are numerous ifs and caveats, the shorter a handgun barrel is, the lower the velocity of any given bullet. A very rough rule of thumb is that a handgun will lose 50 feet per second velocity for each inch lost in barrel length. The Springfield Armory XD-S has a 3.3 inch barrel, so when compared to a full size gun with a five inch barrel, you might see velocity for any given ammunition reduced by as much as 80 to 100 feet per second. So, when fired from a shorter barrel, a bullet designed to expand properly at 1,100 feet per second may not expand at all when traveling at 1,000 feet per second. Conversely, a bullet designed to expand properly at 1,000 feet per second may over-expand, and not penetrate enough, when fired at 1,100 feet per second. Is this bad? No, just different.

With the huge popularity of compact pistols similar to the XD-S, some ammunition companies, like Speer have designed ammunition optimized for proper performance in shorter barrels. For example, rather than designing a bullet to expand at a desired rate when traveling 1,100 feet per second, they design bullets to expand at the desired rate when traveling at 1,000 feet per second.

What does all this mean? It's not enough to just buy any old self-defense ammunition off the shelf. You need to carefully choose your ammunition, considering the gun you're buying it for. In my testing, I've found that Speer's Short Barrel ammunition line is an outstanding option for guns like the Springfield Armory XD-S. One caveat to this applies if you have the new XD-S 4.0 9mm model. That has a four inch barrel, so you don't necessarily have to use Short Barrel expanding ammunition. Depending on your choice of ammunition, you may find that the 4.0 model drives a 9mm projectile 40 to 80 feet per second faster than the original 3.3 inch barrel model. That velocity increase should be enough to allow you more ammunition choices.

Let's take a look.

Speer Gold Dot 9mm 124 grain Short Barrel Hollow Point

I wanted to test multiple Speer Short Barrel loads, in multiple calibers, from the same gun. The Springfield Armory XD-S presented the perfect opportunity. Except for caliber, capacity and a very slight weight difference, the .45 ACP and 9mm XD-S are identical.

Almost any bullet will expand almost every time if you just shoot it into water, gelatin or even soaking wet newspaper. I try to replicate some degree of real-world performance, so I always shoot through some type of barrier, like layers of clothing.

The Speer Gold Dot 9mm Short Barrel load performed perfectly with this 9mm XD-S. Expansion was perfect after passing through two layers of leather and 4 layers of fabric.

For the Speer Gold Dot 9mm Short Barrel test, I got somewhat cranky and put two layers of leather and four layers of fabric in front of my super-duper sophisticated soaking newsprint bullet catcher. That's a pretty tough barrier, but when you consider things like jackets and coats, it's more realistic than nothing.

As you can see from the photo, the projectiles expanded perfectly - even with the leather and fabric barrier. Being a bonded design, where the jacket of the projectile is chemically bonded to the interior lead core, none of the bullets came apart. Just what you want.

SPEER GOLD DOT .45 ACP 230 GRAIN SHORT BARREL HOLLOW POINT

I've found that full weight .45 ACP ammunition is tricky when it comes to expansion. Given the "standard" velocity of a 230 grain .45 ACP projectile at somewhere in the neighborhood of 850 to 900 feet per second, expansion is tough. Every few feet per second of velocity matters when you want the metals in a projectile to spread apart as it travels through tissue. Of course, lots of folks don't really care as the .45 ACP is a large and heavy bullet even when it doesn't expand.

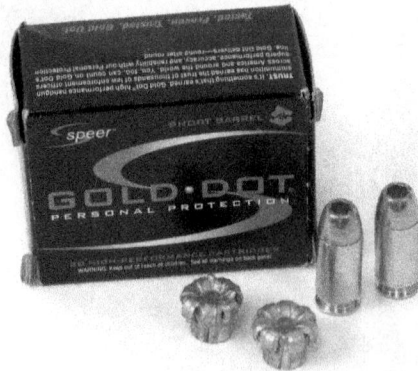

These Speer Gold Dot .45 ACP 230 grain Short Barrel bullets were shot from an XD-S through four layers of denim and still expanded properly.

But hey, we've got modern ammunition technology at our disposal, so I tend to favor ammunition that expands - big .45 bullet or not.

The Speer Gold Dot .45 ACP 230 grain Short Barrel hollow point has advertised velocity of 820 feet per second out of a three-inch barrel gun. The difference is that the projectile itself is designed to expand with less velocity. I fired the bullets shown here through four layers of denim into a big bucket of thoroughly soaked newsprint. As you can see, expansion was right on target. Pun intended. Like all other Gold Dot projectiles, these bullets are bonded so they stay together except under the most extreme circumstances.

WINCHESTER TRAIN AND DEFEND

By the time you read this, you'll be able to get Winchester's new Train and Defend Ammunition. The idea here is simplicity.

New on the market is the Train and Defend offering from Winchester Ammunition.

Under the Train and Defend label, Winchester Ammunition has created two different cartridges for each caliber offering. As you might have guessed, the first option is for training! And the second is for defending. I love the no-brainer idea behind this, but there's a lot more to the story than easy-to-understand box labels.

Winchester created both versions where the bullet weight and recoil are the same. You practice with the less expensive full metal jacket "Train" ammo, then load your gun with the "Defend" hollow point version when carrying or using your gun for home defense.

Both versions are low pressure rounds that have very light recoil, so it's easy to keep on target. The bullets themselves have been designed to expand at lower velocities, so shooting it from a Springfield Armory XD-S will work quite well.

I participated in some testing of this ammunition, firing from short barrel guns, through four layers of clothing and into a gelatin block. The picture below shows the projectiles recovered.

Expansion performance was perfect - even when fired through four layers of clothing per FBI bullet testing protocol.

Winchester Ammunition's Train and Defend is another great option for the XD-S and it's available in both 9mm and .45 ACP calibers.

OTHER AMMUNITION OPTIONS

9mm

If you don't choose a specific short barrel ammunition design, you may want to consider 9mm loads with projectiles on the lighter side of the spectrum. 115 grain or 124 grain loads will provide more velocity out of the 3.3 or 4.0 inch barrel XD-S guns than will the heavier 147 grain 9mm loads. Generally, extra velocity aids consistent expansion.

.45 ACP

Generally speaking, in a gun with a short barrel like the XD-S, I would personally choose a lighter weight .45 ACP bullet in the 160 to 185 grain range. Why? Velocity. All else equal, a lighter weight bullet is easier to push faster. As we discussed earlier in this chapter, velocity aids expansion. So, in theory, a 160 to 185 grain bullet, moving faster, is more likely to expand when shot from a short barrel gun like the XD-S.

We're entering opinion territory here and I'm just sharing my personal preference based on the testing I've done. Non-expanding, full metal jacket .45 ACP ammunition has performed well for over a century, so you may not care whether your particular choice of bullet is an easy expander or not. That's OK. My goal here is to help you make a more informed decision, as all ammunition is not the same.

PRACTICE AMMUNITION

You don't want to shoot the expensive premium self defense ammunition every time you go to the range. At around a buck a shot, your ability to practice might be somewhat hindered by your budget.

In our testing of the Springfield Armory XD-S, we found that this pistol is surprisingly un-picky about ammunition brands. Go to your local gun store, or a reputable online dealer, and pick up some practice ammo of choice. Odds are that it will work just fine in your XD-S.

9mm practice ammunition

Most 9mm practice ammo features a traditional round nose design, so as long as it has standard weight projectiles in the 115 grain, 124 grain or 147 grain range, you should be fine. We shot over a dozen types of factory practice ammunition in the 9mm XD-S and had no problems with feeding or reliability.

.45 ACP practice ammunition

The "standard" .45 ACP practice round is a 230 grain, round nose design traveling somewhere in the 850 feet per second range, give or take. I had no problems with numerous brands of this type of ammo. However, it's easy to find .45 ACP in different designs - with projectiles of different weights and shapes. Just for fun, I even tried practice ammunition with lead semi-wadcutter projectiles. Semi-wadcutter bullets look a little bit like cones with the tops cut off. Even with this odd shape, they worked just fine too. If you have a .45 ACP XD-S, feel free to experiment with different styles of reputable factory ammunition to see what works best for you.

Tips and Tricks for your Springfield Armory XD-S

Let's examine some tips and tricks to help you get more out of your XD-S.

CHANGE THE FRONT SIGHT

The red fiber optic front sight that is pre-installed is pretty nifty. It's highly visible in most conditions. But what if you broke it? Or what if you simply prefer green?

No worries. Changing the front sight tube is an easy one. All you need is a knife or scissors and a lighter. A match will do, but that might leave a little smoky gunk on your sight tube.

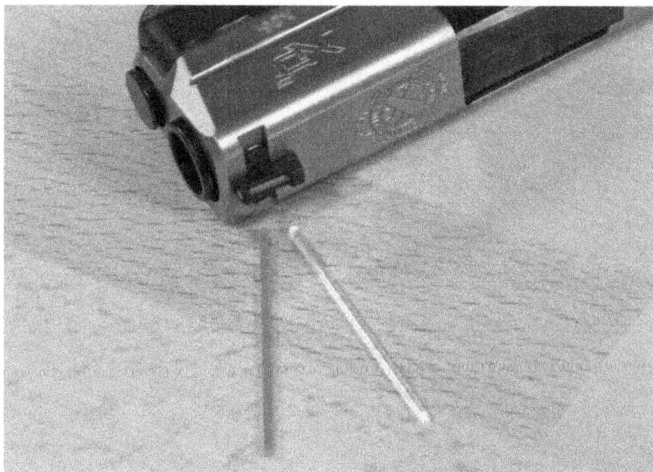

The Springfield Armory XD-S comes with two spare front sight tubes - one red and the other green.

If your original front sight tube got broken, no worries, it's probably already removed. If you want to replace one that's already there with a different color, be prepared for some careful persistence. Removing the existing one is a bit tricky as you don't want to "butch up" the metal on the front sight. I used a craft knife to carefully cut the existing sight tube right in the middle, so each half would fall out the front or back of the front sight housing. Before removing the factory installed fiber-optic tube, be sure to read this whole section completely so you know what's involved with the replacement procedure.

In this section, I'm going to show how to install a new green front sight tube in place of the red one that came factory installed.

The plastic will melt pretty easily - you don't have to get the flame right on it, just close.

Step one is to melt one end of the new sight tube. Applying some heat will make a small "bulb" on the end of the tube, thereby preventing that section from falling through the perfectly sized hole in the front sight housing. Just do one end for now as you'll need to insert the other end through the sight housing.

The unmelted end will slide right through both front and back holes in the front sight housing. The portion you just melted will not fit through the holes.

Slide the unmelted end in first.

The rear portion of the new sight tube is ready to go.

Now you're halfway done. Make sure the tube is pushed through as far as it will go before proceeding to the next step.

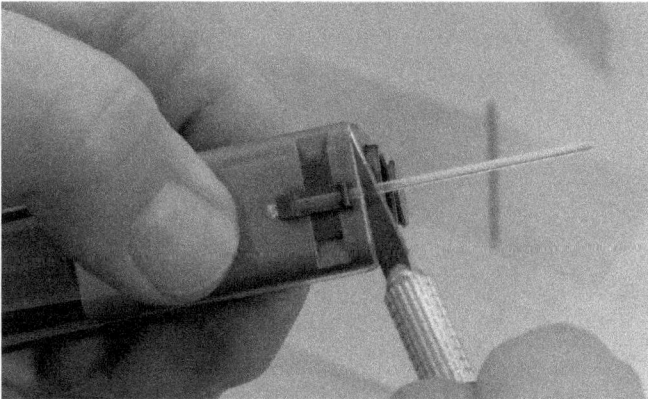

Only leave about 1/16 of an inch extending out of the sight housing.

Now you want to cut the excess from the unmelted end of the new sight tube. Making sure that it's pushed through as far as it will go, use a sharp utility knife to score the new sight tube about 1/16 of an inch from where it exits the sight housing. You don't need to cut it all the way through. If you just score the top, it will break cleanly as shown in the next photo.

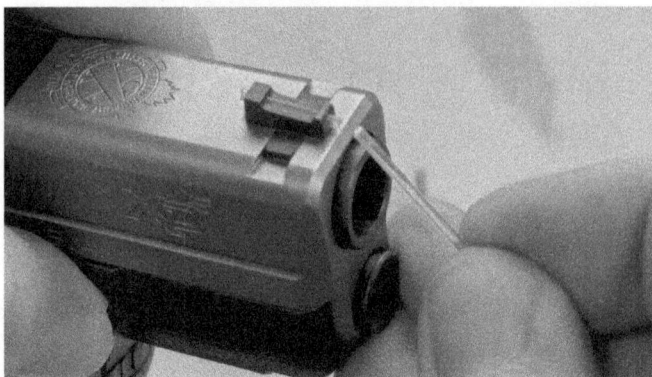

You don't need to cut - a score and break will work just fine.

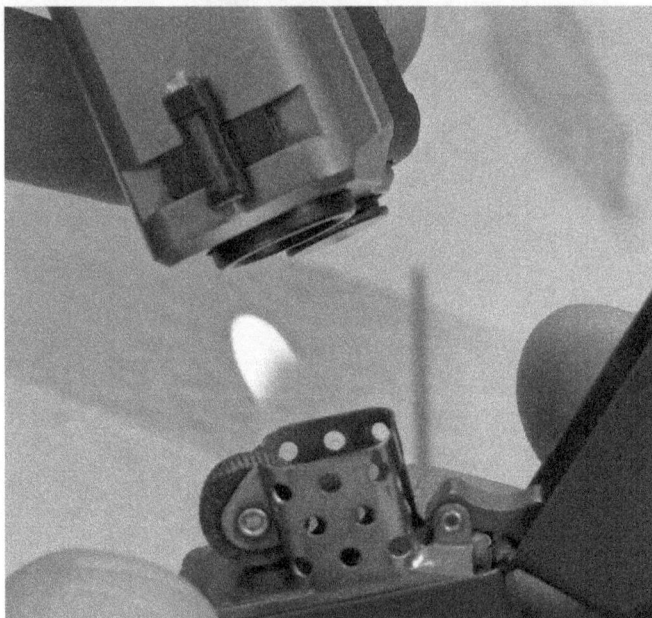

Again, keep the flame away from the tube material so it doesn't get discolored.

Now, use gravity to make sure the tube is seated, and gently melt the end you just scored and broke. This will create a bubble that will "shrink up" to the front sight housing. If you were careful to leave just a bit exposed, you will have a nice tight fit as both ends of the sight tube will be melted against the sight housing.

That's all there is to it!

Voila! Green tube installed!

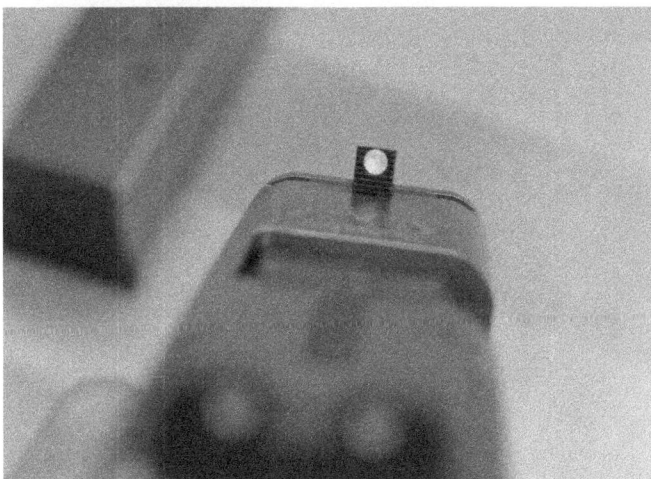

If all went to plan, you should see something like this.

SIGHT ADJUSTMENT

In all likelihood, the factory installed sights will be set properly when you get your Springfield Armory XD-S. If for some reason the gun consistently shoots right or left (windage adjustment) of where you want, both front and rear sights are adjustable. You won't have to worry about up and down (elevation) adjustment as it would be truly shocking if the sights weren't right for most any ammo at distances appropriate for shooting your XD-S.

Before making any sight adjustments, be sure to have someone else shoot your gun. The vast majority of "sight alignment" problems are a result of the shooter, not the gun. No offense intended. It's better to be really, really sure before adjusting your sights. With a small gun like the Springfield Armory XD-S, pulling the gun off target while pressing the trigger is very easy to do.

If you do find that you need to make a sideways adjustment, no problem. While you can move either the front or rear sight to get the desired result, I think moving the rear sight only is easier. On the XD-S, the rear sight has a much larger surface to work with.

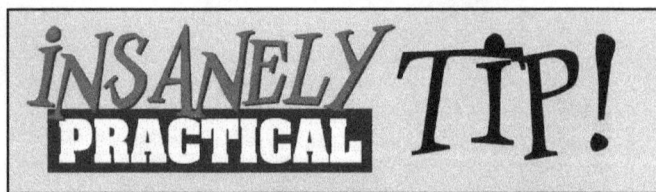

ADJUSTING THE REAR SIGHT

It's easy to remember which way to move the rear sight when you make adjustments. If you want the bullet to hit more to the right, move the rear sight to the right. If you want the bullet to hit more to the left, then push the rear sight a bit to the left.

The easiest way to move the rear sight is using a sight adjustment tool. These tools are kind of like those medieval torture machines with hand cranks. You mount the slide in the device and crank a pusher rod that gradually presses the rear sight one way or the other. You can buy these at places like Brownells.com.

But I'm going to assume you don't have this tool, as most people don't. Adjusting rear sights is not something you do on a regular basis unless you're a gunsmith. Which leads to the second option - taking your XD-S to a local gunsmith or gun shop who does have one of those nifty tools.

The home remedy for sight adjustment is a hard piece of wood and a hammer. You can also use a brass punch, but that can leave discoloration on the rear sight body, so a small block of wood is a little safer.

The rear sight will move back and forth - with a "gentle" nudge.

Recall Information

On August 28, 2013, Springfield Armory issued a recall on both 9mm and .45 ACP models of the XD-S. As the XD-S 4.0 model was released after the recall fix was implemented, you do not have to worry about checking your 4.0 model.

According to Springfield Armory:

> *Springfield has determined that under exceptionally rare circumstances, some 3.3 XD-S™ 9mm and .45ACP caliber pistols could experience an unintended discharge during the loading process when the slide is released, or could experience a double-fire when the trigger is pulled once. The chance of these conditions existing is exceptionally rare, but if they happen, serious injury or death could occur.*

It's important to note that this recall is voluntary, and as of the date of publication, no mishaps or injuries have been reported.

If you recently bought your XD-S in new condition from a dealer, chances are that your gun was manufactured with the recall repairs already implemented. If you've owned it for a while, or bought a used model, you need to check to make sure your gun has been updated.

The first thing to do is to check your gun serial number. If your serial number falls within the affected ranges, you need to determine whether repairs have already been performed on your pistol.

> *Springfield 3.3 XD-S™ 9mm pistols - serial numbers between XS900000 and XS938700*

> *Springfield 3.3 XD-S™ .45ACP pistols - serial numbers between XS500000 and XS686300.*

Fortunately, there's an easy way to determine if an XD-S has the latest parts, with no disassembly required. Just look at the grip safety on your XD-S. If it has been updated with the recall repairs, you will see a roll pin that goes all the way through the grip safety from side to side as this picture shows.

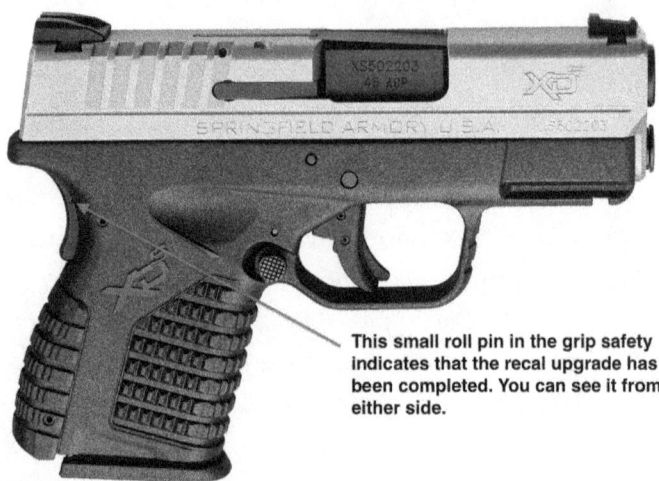

This small roll pin in the grip safety indicates that the recal upgrade has been completed. You can see it from either side.

If your XD-S has already been upgraded with the recall fix, you'll see a small pin in the grip safety as shown here.

WHAT IF YOUR GUN NEEDS RECALL SERVICE?

Springfield Armory has set up a dedicated web site that has the latest information on the recall and repair procedures. We're mentioning it here to help spread the word in the interest of safety, but always rely on the most current information supplied directly from Springfield Armory. If your gun needs service, check this website for detailed instructions:

www.springfieldrecall.com

At time of this writing, the process was easy. Just click on the Get Started link on the recall website for return instructions and shipping label. As your gun is going directly for repair, and being sent back to you, there is no need to ship your gun through an Federal Firearms License (FFL) dealer. You will need to take your packaged gun to a FedEx location instead of an unattended drop box. When your pistol is repaired, Springfield Armory will be able to ship it straight back to you, but an adult signature will be required for delivery.

SHOULD YOU PARTICIPATE IN THE RECALL?

Yes! Gun manufacturers do things like this, when necessary, out of an abundance of caution. As we stated earlier, there have been no injuries yet, but you certainly don't want to be the first. Although your gun will likely perform just fine forever, there is no reason not to have it inspected and repaired.

Send in your gun. You might be inconvenienced for a short time, but will have a lifetime of safe operation as a result.

Gun Safety Rules

Buying a gun is a major responsibility - one that requires that you place safety first and foremost in your plans. As you'll see by the four rules of gun safety outlined in this section, safety rules are often redundant - you have to break more than one for something to go tragically wrong. Learn these rules. Make your friends and family learn them. Make sure every new shooter you take to the range understands these rules. And have fun!

> *"Carrying a gun is not "about the swagger." I own a lawnmower, too, but I don't fantasize about cutting the grass."*
>
> Mike Mollenhour, frequent shooter, an everyday lawyer, an ex-soldier, and a soon-to-be-world famous author. He exercises the First Amendment about the Second Amendment, liberty, and national defense blogging at www.virtualmilitia.com

RULE 1: A GUN IS ALWAYS LOADED!

Yes. Always. Like Lindsay Lohan and the questions on 60 Minutes. Even when it's not.

Every year we hear about people who are accidentally shot with 'unloaded' guns.

"I thought it was unloaded!"

"I'm sure I unloaded it last time I put it away!"

"It wasn't loaded before!"

"Maybe I was loaded last time I unloaded it!"

Of course, a gun is not technically always loaded. But the intent of Rule 1 is to **treat a gun as if it's always loaded**. If you treat a gun like it is loaded, you tend to change your behavior in terms of how you handle that gun.

Hopefully you won't check out the sights by aiming it at someone.

And of course you won't pull the trigger, unless you're actually ready to fire the gun at a safe target. More on that in a minute.

And certainly you won't do anything else careless with it.

Rule 1 is first on the priority list, because it's Rule 1, but also because it covers a lot of safety ground. Treating a gun like it is loaded and ready to fire has a fantastic ripple effect that makes everyone around safer.

So take it seriously. Pretend that a gun is loaded every single time you look at it or touch it. Pretty soon you'll start believing that it IS actually loaded. Even when you look, and verify that it's not, you'll want to look again to make sure. This is a good thing. Never ignore a gut feeling to check the status of a gun just one more time to be sure.

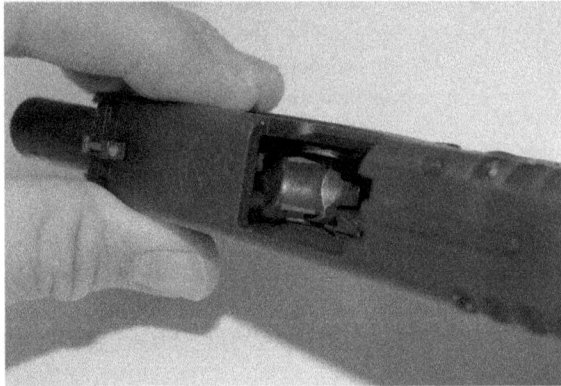

Is this obviously "empty" XD-S loaded? YES! A gun is ALWAYS loaded!

I like to have some fun with this when teaching new shooters the safety rules. Not for fun's sake alone, but to really drive home the point. Immediately after telling them Rule 1, the gun is always loaded, I pick up a gun, point it in a safe direction, and open gun's action to show them. It's empty of course, but I don't tell them that. I ask them if the gun is loaded. It's even better when both kids and adults are present in this new shooter orientation. Almost without fail, the kids look at me with an odd puzzled look for a second, then respond "Yes! It IS loaded!" Kids are much better students than adults. They love getting this trick question right! Adults tend to score about 50% on this pop quiz. About half of them cautiously inspect the gun, then tell me that the gun appears to be unloaded. We all have a quick laugh when I tell them, "WRONG! It's ALWAYS loaded!" Then they get it.

So be creative when talking about the rules of gun safety with others. You can have fun teaching people to be safe - and just maybe they'll remember!

RULE 2: KEEP YOUR FINGER OFF THE TRIGGER UNTIL READY TO FIRE!

Modern guns are safe mechanical devices. While you should never rely on any mechanical device for safety - as anything can fail - it's really, really unlikely that a modern gun will fire without someone or something pressing its trigger. Most guns can be dropped or even thrown with no risk of firing. Others require one - or more - safety devices to be deactivated before a trigger pull will even allow the gun to fire. So more than likely, when you hear a story about a "gun just going off" you can generally assume that someone, somehow, moved that trigger.

All of these are reasons why Rule 2 is so important. If your finger is not on the trigger, it sure is hard to inadvertently press it!

Unless you're about to fire, keep your trigger finger placed like this. Not only is it safe, it let's others around you easily see that you're being safe.

Rule 2 might be the hardest habit for new shooters to cement in their memory.

It's a hook after all. That makes a perfect finger rest. You have opposable digits that are designed to grasp things. All of your available fingers prefer to move together in the same direction, so when the middle, ring and pinky finger close around a gun grip, the index finger wants to close also. The natural and instinctive motion when picking up a gun is to grasp it with your finger on the trigger.

It's a massive temptation. And a terribly unsafe habit that needs to be broken through practice and repetition. Scientists say that it takes 1,000 to 2,000 repetitions of an action to firmly establish an automatic habit in your brain. The same concept applies to learning how to keep your finger off the trigger.

It's fairly easy to train someone not to put their finger on the trigger when they pick up a gun. A few reminders generally solves that problem. But there is far more to developing really safe trigger discipline. It has to become an ingrained reflex no matter what the scenario. Immediately after their last shot, does that finger come off the trigger? When changing magazines, does the finger come off the trigger? Does the finger come off between the last shot and setting the gun back down on the table or putting it back in a holster? What if you have to move during the middle of shooting? Will your finger automatically come off the trigger? What about if you are interrupted or startled while shooting? Will your brain still remember to tell you finger to back off?

So training yourself, or others, to keep the finger off the trigger until ready to fire is a chore. Reminding someone over and over to get their finger off the trigger can ruffle some feathers. But you can make the training process respectful, un-intimidating and even fun. When taking new shooters to the range, I tell them (with a smile of course) that I'm going to have to remind them frequently to remove their trigger finger. With some discussion beforehand, no one gets defensive when you have to nudge them at the range. You can also have your family and friends train you. Just ask them to watch you shoot while focusing on your trigger finger.

RULE 3: NEVER POINT A GUN AT ANYTHING YOU'RE NOT WILLING TO DESTROY!

Besides, pistol whipping can be a great alternative.

Nah, just kidding!

We like to keep things simple around here. You'll hear lots of terminology variations that describe rule 3.

"Never cover anything you're not willing to destroy!"

"Don't muzzle anything you're not prepared to shoot!"

"Always keep the gun pointed in a safe direction!"

"Never let the muzzle cover anything you're not willing to destroy!"

"Point the muzzle only at non-targets!"

While there are a number of ways to describe Rule 3, we like the direct approach. After all, not everyone understands the terminology of "covering." To a novice shooter, "covering" or "muzzling" could have meanings more related to group hugs than where a gun is pointed.

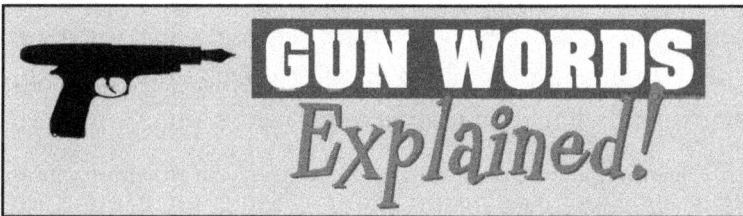

GUN WORDS Explained!

MUZZLE

A muzzle is the fiery end of a gun. It's where the bullet comes out. It's the hole in the end that you never, ever, ever want to be looking at.

If you want to get technical, it's the front opening of a gun barrel. The barrel as a whole contains the rapidly burning propellant gases and guide the bullet on its path. Since we're talking about muzzles, it's a good time to mention the other end of the barrel. Located in the back, it is referred to as the breach. Breach, back. Muzzle, front. Simple right?

The key word in Rule 3 is NEVER. According to the Random House Dictionary, the word "never" has two definition components. Not ever or at no time. And to no extent or degree. The "to no extent or degree" part is actually the most important when considered with Rule 3.

It's fairly obvious that you should not stand around and keep a gun pointed at someone or something that should not be shot. It's far less obvious to think about "pointing" as the act of allowing the muzzle to face someone or something for the briefest instant. It's still considered "pointing" if that muzzle simply moves across something you don't intend to shoot.

I like to tell shooters to think about the muzzle of a gun as a mega-powered, laser-beam, light saber of doom with no "off" button. Sort of like those big spotlights at used car dealerships. This destructive beam continues in (mostly) a straight line from the gun muzzle to *infinity - and beyond*. This beam waves around wherever the gun muzzle points - all the time. So if the muzzle "points" at something, even for a microsecond, that certain something is destroyed.

The muzzle beam of destruction is activated whenever you touch a gun. It doesn't matter if it's in a gun store, a show, at the range, in your home, or in a gun holster. When you touch it, the beam turns on and you have to watch every single movement for every single instant. As you move the gun around, what does that beam cross? Or, if you set a gun on the table to do something to it, where is it pointing? I see this scenario at the range all the time. If there is a malfunction, people will set the gun down to work on it, not realizing it's pointed at the shooter next to them.

It may sound obvious as you read this, but Rule 3 includes your own body and extremities - not just those of others. Consider where the muzzle points as you pick up a gun, inspect it, put it away, draw it from a holster or whatever. Be especially cautious of muzzling your arm or leg as they tend to move around and have a great probability of being in the wrong place at the wrong time!

RULE 4: BE SURE OF YOUR TARGET AND WHAT'S BEHIND IT!

Bullets tend to go through things. That's one of the reason they are so good at being bullets.

The key part of Rule 4 is the "what's behind it" part. There are two reasons that you need to carefully consider what's behind the target.

First, your bullet may go right through the target and continue out the back, still traveling at great velocity. If it's still moving after passing through the first target, it's still dangerous.

Second, unlike James Bond and The Lone Ranger, it's possible for us mortals to miss the primary target once in a while. And if you miss, there is a zero percent chance that your target will stop your bullet.

These bullets passed right through stone floor tile with enough energy left over to plow 10 inches into wet newspaper.

Rule 4 uses the words "be sure" for a very good reason. Unless you are absolutely positive about what's behind your target, don't shoot. Being "pretty sure" isn't good enough when it comes to gun safety. If your view is obscured, don't shoot. Be sure.

HALF-COCKED
BY MYGUNCULTURE.COM

GUN FREE ZONE

IN A BOLD COST CUTTING MOVE, THE WHITE HOUSE ANNOUNCED PLANS TO ELIMINATE THE SECRET SERVICE IN FAVOR OF MORE EFFECTIVE SECURITY MEASURES.

Parting Shots

BE SAFE AND HAVE FUN!

We hope you enjoyed reading this book. It's intended to help relieve some of the apprehension and stress related to buying, maintaining and shooting the Springfield Armory XD-S.

Most importantly, pay attention to the safety tips. Shooting is an incredibly safe pastime when people faithfully obey the four rules of gun safety.

Now go have fun!

One more thing. Stay in touch by subscribing to our email list. We send updates on books, shooting tips and other fun news once a week, with no spam ever!

Sign up here: mygunculture.com/email

ABOUT MY GUN CULTURE

My Gun Culture is a half-cocked but right-on-target look at the world of shooting and all things related. If you want to learn, with a laugh, about guns, shooting products, personal defense, competition, industry news and the occasional Second Amendment issue, check us out at MyGunCulture.com.

Our literary assault team has developed contacts and access to the very depths of the shooting industry to bring you current and useful information with a side order of chuckle. From how-to's to interviews of industry figures to product reviews, we'll continue to bring you the latest and greatest from the industry.

Visit us at:

Mygunculture.com

www.facebook.com/mygunculture

www.twitter.com/mygunculture

www.pinterest.com/mygunculture

ABOUT THE AUTHOR

Tom McHale was born helpless, hungry and shooting-deprived. He later discovered the joys of collecting and shooting guns, reloading ammunition and writing about his adventures with a healthy dose of fun.

Tom's career has been diverse, bordering on dysfunctional, with most of it spent leading marketing teams for a variety of technology companies including Microsoft and more than a couple of high-tech startups. He's finally seen the light and given up the corporate life to pursue his passion of creating educational, but slightly crazy, content related to guns, shooting, concealed carry and self defense. His most recent project is publishing a series of informative books under the Insanely Practical Guides brand. You can learn more at InsanelyPracticalGuides.com.

Drop me an email at: tom@insanelypracticalguides.com

ALSO FROM INSANELY PRACTICAL GUIDES...

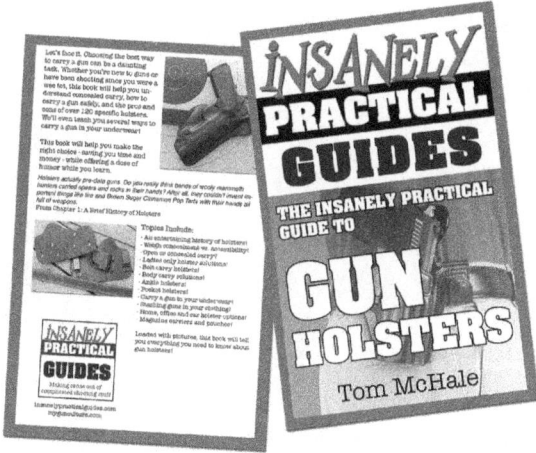

Choosing the best way to carry a gun can be a daunting task. Whether you're new to guns or have been shooting since you were a wee tot, this book can help you understand concealed carry methods, how to carry a gun safely, and the relative pros and cons of over 120 specific holster models. This book will help you make the right choice - saving you time and money - while offering a dose of humor while you learn.

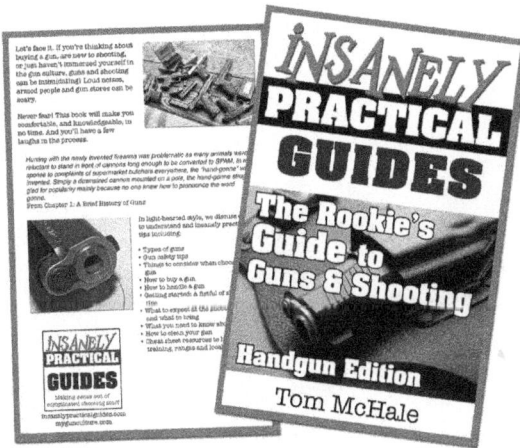

If you're thinking about buying a gun, are new to shooting, or just haven't immersed yourself in the gun culture, guns and shooting can be intimidating! Loud noises, armed people and gun stores can be scary. Never fear! This book will make you comfortable, and knowledgeable, in no time. And you'll have a few laughs in the process.

Find information on our books at <u>InsanelyPracticalGuides.com</u>

www.ingramcontent.com/pod-product-compliance
Lightning Source LLC
Chambersburg PA
CBHW031321040426
42443CB00005B/175